WOMEN AND
POLITICAL PARTICIPATION

WOMEN AND POLITICAL PARTICIPATION

Cultural Change in the Political Arena

Second Edition

M. Margaret Conway
UNIVERSITY OF FLORIDA

Gertrude A. Steuernagel
KENT STATE UNIVERSITY

David W. Ahern
UNIVERSITY OF DAYTON

A Division of Congressional Quarterly Inc.
Washington, D.C.

CQ Press
1255 22nd Street, N.W., Suite 400
Washington, D.C. 20037

(202) 729-1900; toll-free, 1-866-4CQ-PRESS (1-866-427-7737)

www.cqpress.com

⊗ The paper used in this publication exceeds the requirements of the American National Standard for Information Sciences—Permanence of Paper for Printed Library Materials, ANSI Z39.48-1992.

Printed and bound in the United States of America

08 07 06 05 04   5 4 3 2 1

Cover design: TGD Communications, Alexandria, Va.

Library of Congress Cataloging-in-Publication Data

Conway, M. Margaret (Mary Margaret)
    Women and political participation : cultural change in the political arena /
M. Margaret Conway, Gertrude A. Steuernagel, David W. Ahern.— 2nd ed.
        p. cm.
    Includes bibliographical references and index.
    ISBN 1-56802-925-X (alk. paper)
    1. Women in politics—United States. I. Steuernagel, Gertrude A. II.
Ahern, David W. III. Title.

HQ1236.5.U6C65 2004
306.2'082—dc22

                                            2004015497

For Robin and Jean Gibson
M.M.C.

For Scott and Sky—the heart of me
G.S.

In memory of my mother, Janet Ahern
D.A.

Contents

Tables and Figures

FIGURES

Preface

This book about women's political participation in the United States focuses on the effects of cultural change on gender roles and the impact of role perception on women's political attitudes and political behavior.

In many ways, the story of women's political participation is the story of cultural change. Barbara Boxer's description of her awakening political interests illustrates this. Barbara Boxer was not politically active until the assassination of Robert Kennedy spurred her to action. She won election to the U.S. Senate two decades later. She remarked: "[My husband] must have felt like he married Debbie Reynolds and woke up with Eleanor Roosevelt!"[1]

At any point in our history, culture influences our perception of women. This happens in part through the presentation of images. Any culture presents a variety of images of women, and these images affect people's thinking. A culture can present no images of women as leaders, thus sending a message that women cannot lead; or it can present images of women as religious leaders but not as political leaders, suggesting that some areas of leadership are open to women but not others.

But cultural images evolve, and in doing so they often reflect the confusion that results when society experiences change—such as in popular notions of what women appropriately can and cannot do. For example, the "waif look," which was popular among fashion models in the early 1990s, suggested that women were childlike and frail. In the meantime, women were winning seats in Congress in the election of 1992. The waifs may have been a cultural response to women's increasing involvement in political affairs. The image may even have served as a safety valve for some of the dissent and anxiety surrounding such a major cultural change. What is clear is that this image of women coexisted with, rather than replaced, the newly emerging image of women as political activists.

In this book we explore women's political participation in the context of cultural change; we believe that this context is critical to understanding women and political participation. This new edition includes more discussion of feminism, particularly third wave feminism, as well as an expanded discussion of the agents of socialization that incorporates treatment of the effects of race, ethnicity, and class on women's political socialization. Chapter 1 is an introduction to women's status in a liberal culture and a survey of women's political participation from colonial times to the passage of women's suffrage in 1920. Women's notions of gender roles, appropriate behavior and attitudes, and gender identity are the subjects of Chapter 2, which includes a discussion of childhood and adult political learning, with particular emphasis on acculturation and political socialization. In Chapter 3 we examine the gender gap in political attitudes and historical trends in women's political attitudes. Chapter 4 is an analysis of the relationship between trends in women's political attitudes and in their social attitudes, the influence of changing cultural images of women, and changes in people's political attitudes. In Chapter 5 we consider the gender gap in voting, historical trends in women's voting behavior, and the effects of changes in women's roles on their turnout to vote and their vote choice. Chapter 6 focuses on the cultural construction of images of women as political leaders (as members of political parties, in political campaigns, and as officeholders) and the implications of these images for women's political leadership. The impact of women's participation on politics and public policy is assessed in Chapter 7.

This book will be of interest to students of U.S. politics and women's studies. We hope it helps to strengthen a movement, begun in the 1970s, to make gender a serious subject of study in political science; academic discourse contributes to the cultural construction of images of women. Gender has always been a politically relevant subject, even though political scientists have sometimes ignored it; and American women have always been politically involved, even when society tried to stop them.

An effort has been made to make the material in this book accessible to students, with suggestions for further reading and Web sites for those wishing to pursue particular topics. Because the academic literature often lags behind the media and the culture in identifying cultural change, and because we wanted to put a human face on cultural change, we have included stories from real life to demonstrate that cultural change can affect individual lives often before it is recognized as a trend by analysts.

Some of the data used in this book were made available by the InterUniversity Consortium for Political and Social Research. The data for the American National Election Studies were collected by the Center for Political Studies at the University of Michigan, under grants funded by the National Science Foundation. Neither the original collectors of the data nor the consortium bear any responsibility for the analyses or interpretations presented here.

M. Margaret Conway gratefully acknowledges the research support provided by the Robin and Jean Gibson Term Professorship, College of Liberal Arts, University of Florida, during the 1995–1996 academic year.

The authors acknowledge the contributions of Brenda Carter, Charisse Kiino, Colleen Ganey, and Belinda Josey of CQ Press and of Molly Lohman, an excellent manuscript editor.

We would like to thank all our students and fellow women and politics faculty, including the anonymous reviewers of the first edition, whose comments have helped us to prepare this new edition. Their informed participation has guided our revisions and reaffirmed our commitment to providing a text that meets their expectations and needs.

NOTES

1. Barbara Boxer with Nicole Boxer, *Strangers in the Senate: Politics and the New Revolution of Women in America* (Washington, D.C.: National Press Books, 1994), 69.

CHAPTER 1

Women, Culture, and Political Participation

Eleanora Tomec, born in Pittsburgh in 1910, was the only one of seven siblings to survive past the age of five.[1] She began to work as a secretary immediately after graduating from the eighth grade, but her Slovenian immigrant parents encouraged her to continue her education. She obtained a high school diploma by attending night school and then enrolled in a few college classes. So eager were her parents for her to be part of their adopted homeland, however, that they refused to teach her to speak Slovenian, insisting that she speak English "like a good American girl."

Tomec became engaged to a local man, and they married in 1945 after he returned from military service in World War II. Thus she was thirty-five at the time of her marriage, not twenty or twenty-one, the typical ages of women who married for the first time in 1945.[2] The year of her marriage was also the year when the divorce rate reached its highest level of the century.[3] Tomec continued to work as a secretary until their first child, a girl, was born in 1946. Tomec was fairly typical in this respect. The birth rate in 1946, 23.3 births per 1,000 people, was the highest since 1921.[4] Her second daughter was born in 1948. Both Tomec and her husband felt they had to "keep trying" until they had the son they so wanted. Despite her age, Tomec had a third child, a boy, in 1951. She remained out of the paid work force until he entered kindergarten, then returned to work as a secretary part-time. By 1960 she was working full-time. In that year, 49.9 percent of the women in her age group, forty-five to fifty-four, were in the labor force on a full- or part-time basis, compared with 95.7 percent of the men in that age group.[5] Although Tomec was somewhat typical in this regard in 1960, she had not been so earlier in her working life. In 1940, when Tomec was thirty, 95.2 percent of the men ages twenty-five to thirty-four were in the labor force; only 32.9 percent of women could say the same.[6]

Tomec's earnings were earmarked for her children's education. All three graduated from college, but she and her husband had made certain that their son went to a prestigious school, whereas the daughters, both of whom had academic records superior to that of their brother, attended a nearby state university. The daughter who challenged the justice of this decision was told by her father that she was fortunate to attend any college since the family "had a boy to educate."

Tomec died of breast cancer in 1974, two years after a radical mastectomy and radiation therapy. Doctors did not discuss treatment options with her or her family, and the biopsy and surgery were performed in a single operation. She lived to see her children graduate from college but died before the births of her three grandchildren. In 1974, 26.8 of every 100,000 American women died of breast cancer.[7]

Many cultural changes occurred during Tomec's lifetime. She was born ten years before passage of the Nineteenth Amendment guaranteed the right to vote for all American women; the education she received was limited but exceeded that of her parents. Although she spent her working life in a traditional female occupation, she was one of the few women in her neighborhood who worked full-time while her children were young. During World War II Tomec continued to work as a secretary, showing no interest in better-paying defense jobs such as that held by "Rosie the Riveter." The era that encompassed most of her working years was one in which women's status had not yet become a public policy issue. The Equal Pay Act of 1963 and Title VII of the Civil Rights Act of 1964 (which outlawed sexual discrimination in employment) thus had little impact on her life. A devout Catholic, she opposed abortion but was too ill at the time to take much interest in the *Roe v. Wade* decision (1973). When she detected the lump in her breast and went to have it examined, she did not question the doctor's decision that, were the biopsy positive, a radical mastectomy should be performed immediately. When she awoke from the anesthesia, she was told that the lump had been malignant and that the surgery had already been performed.

Politically, Tomec like her parents and husband, was a Democrat. Unlike many women at that time, she voted regularly. Adlai Stevenson, the Democratic presidential candidate in 1952 and 1956, was her political hero, although his divorce troubled her. She supported John F. Kennedy, the Democratic presidential candidate in 1960, in large part because he was a Catholic. Tomec was not a joiner and belonged to no community groups. She was never involved in any form of legal or illegal protest activity, but she did support her children in their antiwar activities. One of her daughters claimed that she knew that the United States' involvement in Vietnam had lost popular support when she overheard her mother bragging to her father that, of all the children of the Saturday morning regulars at Teresa Eppolito's House of Beauty, one of theirs had been the first in town to march in Washington, D.C.

Politically, Tomec identified with party and faith, not gender. She wanted her daughters to be able to make choices about education and career but often felt distanced from both "girls," as she continued to call them throughout her life. It was Tomec's commitment, emotionally and financially, to her daughters' education that made possible their college degrees. She both gloried in and despaired over their independence. In her mind, her older daughter's wedding assumed mythic proportions because it was the only sign that either of the two young women was interested in leading a traditional lifestyle. If Tomec was at all aware of the women's movement, she never made mention of it to her family.

The story of Tomec and her family is also the story of American women's political participation, for both are about personal and cultural change. Culture can be defined as a core of traditional ideas, practices, and technology shared by a people." [8] This focus on culture is based on the idea that what matters to individuals—what affects their political attitudes, for example—is learned through their interaction with the people and institutions they encounter throughout their lives.[9]

Tomec played many roles during her lifetime: dutiful daughter, efficient employee, loyal wife and companion, and responsible mother. Both she and her roles changed in that period. All in all, politics had little meaning for her. This is not to say, however, that she had no political opinions. Each of her three children was educated in a parochial school, and she was intent on ensuring that state and local governments not be involved in administrating these schools. She acknowledged that she and her husband would have to pay their property taxes to support the public schools while also paying tuition for private schools. Although she lived most of her life in segregated white neighborhoods, she supported integration. She opposed the war in Vietnam and told her family that should her son be drafted, she would want him to flee to Canada. Tomec thought that homosexuality was a perversion, marriage was forever, and the United States was the best place in the world to live and raise a family. She died before environmentalism became a household word. She had no objection to paying taxes to support poor families, but she believed that too many people were too lazy to work.

What did political participation mean to Tomec? She viewed herself as a good citizen because she tried to stay informed, and she voted in primaries and general elections. Occasionally she would donate money to a Democratic candidate. But she never wrote a letter to a governmental official or put a political bumper sticker on her car.

WOMEN'S STATUS IN A LIBERAL CULTURE

There are many ways to describe the culture that influenced Tomec and her fellow citizens. It is most commonly defined as "liberal." A liberal culture values individuality, freedom, and equality. Politically, it embraces democracy; economically, it is based on capitalism. What people in a liberal culture do with their lives is their concern, so long as their actions do not harm others or infringe on others' rights.[10] Government is supposed to act as a referee and is not supposed to give special treatment to any person or group. A liberal culture, however, does not require continuous, intense political participation, defined as "those activities of citizens that attempt to influence the structure of government, the selection of government authorities, or the policies of government." [11] What is required is that the right to participate politically not be abridged. From this perspective, a liberal culture does not necessarily consider lack of political participation as negative.

Women's status in this liberal culture has changed over time, as has the culture itself.[12] In part, these changes in the lives of women are a result of the organized women's movement, which challenged the rigid roles assigned to women and expanded women's options in such areas as education and employment. The contrasts between Tomec's life and the lives of her daughters are indicative of these changes. Although Tomec worked throughout much of her adulthood, her job took second place to that of her husband; she thought of her work as a job and of her husband's work as a career. When he had to relocate because of work Tomec moved with him; it was taken for granted that she would take time away from work for child rearing. During the time she stayed home with the children she was not a member of the paid work force. As a result, she never accumulated enough time in any one job to earn a pension. Tomec's older daughter left a promising career upon the birth of her first child. Throughout her marriage she assumed the traditional roles of homemaker and mother. Unlike Tomec, however, she did consider alternatives. She remained out of the work force for almost twenty years, reentering only at the time of her divorce. Although she had a college degree, her skills had become obsolete and her first job on returning to the work force was a low-paying clerical one. The younger daughter, in contrast, worked continually after completing graduate school. She married late and had a child late in her childbearing years, but neither event caused her to leave the work force for more than two weeks. Both she and her husband viewed child rearing as a shared responsibility.

Tomec and her daughters had different ideas about work, marriage, and motherhood. The daughters had educational opportunities that were unavailable to Tomec. The younger daughter raised her child at a time when there were far more child care options than her mother or sister could ever have imagined. Divorce for Tomec was never an option, but it was for her older daughter. Tomec can be said to have been more accepting of a patriarchal society than were her daughters. Although a liberal culture stresses autonomy and self-determination, they have been relative concepts, not always applicable in theory or practice to everyone. Before the Civil War, for example, many white Americans justified the "peculiar institution" of slavery as the best policy for both whites and blacks. Even in the Constitution of the United States, slaves were originally counted as three-fifths of a person for purposes of taxation and representation. And after women were legally recognized as persons, they were not always able to take full advantage of the opportunities of the liberal culture. Women's responsibilities with regard to home and children, for example, could interfere with their ability to act as autonomous beings in the workplace. Tomec was never denied the right to vote because of her sex, but her life took a certain shape because she was a woman.

WOMEN AND CULTURAL CHANGE

Both Tomec and her daughters were at some time part of the nation's work force, and this is the trend for all American women. In 2001, 60 percent of

American women worked outside the home; married women were almost as likely as single women to be employed, and the rates of employment for black married women were higher than for white married women.[13] Approximately five decades earlier, in 1950, only 34 percent of American women were in the work force, and married women were less likely than single women to be employed.[14] Tomec's younger daughter, who continued to work after her child was born, is part of another trend. In 2001 more than 60 percent of all women with children under the age of six worked full- or part-time.[15] Women's areas of employment have not changed as much as have the percentages of women who are employed. Tomec spent all of her working years as a secretary. In 2002, 98 percent of all secretaries were female. In 1940, 988,081 women and 68,805 men were employed as stenographers, typists, or secretaries.[16] Tomec's daughters' occupations reflect the movement of women out of the "pink-collar ghettos," where most women are still employed. Her older daughter was a computer programmer, a profession that in 2001 was 30 percent female. Her younger daughter became a university professor, a profession that in 2001 was 36 percent female.[17]

Tomec obtained her high school diploma in night school and earned a few college credits. In respect to education, Tomec was fairly typical of her peers. In 1940 the median number of school years completed by someone in Tomec's age group (thirty to thirty-four) was 9.5. For males the figure was 9.2 and for females 9.9. In that same age group in 1940, women were more likely than men to have completed high school, but men were more likely than women to have four or more years of college. Interestingly, in that year women were more likely than men to have one to three years of college (as did Tomec).[18] Her older daughter earned a bachelor's degree and her younger daughter earned bachelor's, master's, and doctoral degrees. Again, the trend in Tomec's family reflects the broader cultural trend. In 2000 more women than men were enrolled in college, more women than men earned bachelor degrees, and more women than men earned master's degrees. Men continue to earn more doctoral degrees than women. More and more women are earning degrees in traditionally male fields such as engineering and business. Although fewer blacks and Hispanics earn bachelor's degrees than do whites, the rates for black women and men are similar, both around 16 percent, and Hispanic women and men both earn degrees at a rate of 10 percent. Asians and Pacific Islanders are more likely than any other racial or ethnic group to earn college degrees, although the rate for men in this group is close to 48 percent, while for women it is close to 41 percent.[19]

Women's political participation has both caused and been affected by cultural change. Women's efforts to change a culture that denied them the right to participate fully in political activities are the subject of the following section.

WOMEN'S POLITICAL PARTICIPATION:
COLONIAL TIMES TO 1920

Women participated in political activities long before the ratification of the Nineteenth Amendment to the Constitution (1920), which established women's right to vote in all federal, state, and local government elections. During the American Revolution, many women joined the Daughters of Liberty and supported the war effort by providing supplies such as food and clothing to soldiers and by persuading women to boycott goods imported from England. Before the Civil War, many women in the North were active in the abolitionist movement. Their experiences enabled them to gain the organizational and oratorical skills that many would use in the women's suffrage movement. During the nineteenth century, many women participated in other efforts to affect policy, which included campaigns to establish free public education, to improve the working conditions of women employed in factories (in textiles and other industries), and to gain the right for labor unions to organize. Women also formed organizations with such varied goals as providing charity to the impoverished, lobbying the federal government to create widow's and orphan's pensions for survivors of soldiers killed in the Civil War, and obtaining passage of federal and state laws prohibiting children from working in factories and mines.[20]

Women's Political Status Before the Nineteenth Amendment

Under common law, which the colonies' founders brought with them from England, women lost all legal rights when they married.[21] Husband and wife became one legal entity, and the husband exercised legal rights for the couple, including the right to vote. Single women had few legal rights and did not have the right to vote.[22]

In colonial America, women thus did not have a legally established right to vote. Margaret Brent presented one early request for the voting franchise to the Maryland Council in 1647. A wealthy plantation owner,

Brent was also the agent and representative of Lord Baltimore, the proprietor of the Maryland colony, as well as the executor of the estate of Leonard Calvert, the deceased brother of Lord Baltimore. She demanded not one vote, but two—the first because she met the colony's property-owning qualifications for voting, and the second because she was the representative of the estate of Leonard Calvert. She argued that if her request were denied, all proceedings of the Maryland House of Burgesses would be invalid. The Maryland Council was not persuaded and rejected her request.[23]

Abigail Adams of Massachusetts, the wife of John Adams (who later became the second president of the United States), wrote to him in 1787 when he was serving as a member of the convention that was drafting the U.S. Constitution. She requested that "he remember the ladies" and not put unlimited power in the hands of men.[24] But the Constitutional Convention did not consider her request for political rights for women.

Despite the lack of formal enfranchisement of women, in several communities women members of some prominent families did vote until state laws were enacted to prohibit it. For example, women voted in New Jersey until 1807, when political leaders who feared that women's votes would contribute to their opponents' success enacted a state law prohibiting women from voting in elections.[25]

During the nineteenth century, women in a few states obtained the right to vote in school board elections. In recognition of women's role in child rearing, in 1838 Kentucky became the first state to grant women a limited right to vote; it allowed widows in rural districts who had children in school to vote in school board elections.[26] In 1861 Kansas became the second state to grant women the right to vote in school board elections. By 1900 women were eligible to vote in school board elections in twenty-four states.[27]

Nonetheless, women's political and legal rights were restricted in most states during the nineteenth century. This is not to say all people accepted the status quo. In 1845, for example, the Transcendentalist Margaret Fuller authored *Woman in the Nineteenth Century*, which argued that civilization could not advance and neither men nor women could perfect their souls until slavery was abolished and all women and men became full members of society. The extension of political rights began in the frontier states and proceeded very slowly. The first full grant of suffrage to women occurred in 1869, when the drafters of the Wyoming territorial constitution enfranchised women in the hope of attracting more of them to settle in that sparsely populated state. When Wyoming became a state in 1890, its constitution stipulated that women had a right to vote in all elections. By 1918 fifteen states (of which thirteen were western states) had granted women the right to vote in all elections; by 1920 an additional thirteen states had granted women the right to vote only in presidential elections.[28]

Why is the right to vote so important? It provides a mechanism by which citizens may influence both who rules and what public policies they implement. When a group of people with a common concern votes on the basis of that concern and makes its desires known to political candidates, the group may alter both the campaign promises and the performance in office of those who are elected. The right to vote can thus be a powerful weapon for obtaining preferred policy outcomes.[29]

The Struggle for Women's Rights and Passage of the Nineteenth Amendment

The struggle that culminated in congressional passage of the Nineteenth Amendment and its ratification by the states lasted more than a century. The organized campaign for women's suffrage can be traced to the involvement of women in the antislavery movement. Two of the founders of that first women's movement, Elizabeth Cady Stanton and Lucretia Mott, attended an international antislavery convention in London in 1840. Both men and women were there to represent the United States. The convention ruled, however, that the women could not be official delegates and would have to sit in the gallery with the spectators. That incident led Stanton and Mott to spend much of their time in London discussing the legal status and social condition of women; they resolved to work to change them. Both women were married, and Stanton and her large family moved to the small town of Seneca Falls in upstate New York. Because she had almost total responsibility for the daily household and child-rearing tasks (her husband was frequently away on business and she seldom had dependable household help), Stanton had little time to organize a social or political movement.[30]

In 1848 Lucretia Mott and her husband visited friends residing near the Stanton home in Seneca Falls. Stanton and Mott, together with three women friends, decided to call a "convention" to discuss the social, political, and economic conditions of women. They placed a small advertisement in the *Seneca County Courier* inviting others to attend a women's rights meeting at the Methodist Chapel on July 19 and 20, 1848. Only women were asked to attend the first day of the meeting; men were invited to attend the second day. However, men were present on both days, and James Mott was asked to chair the meeting, as none of the women who organized the meeting had such experience.[31] The women organizers drafted a Declaration of Principles, which was largely a paraphrase of the Declaration of Independence. Stanton also drafted a set of resolutions designed to implement the Declaration of Principles. The only resolution that was not passed unanimously was Resolution 9: "Resolved that it is the duty of the women of this country to secure their sacred right to the elective franchise." The idea of the vote for women was so controversial that the resolution passed by only a small margin.[32] Of the sixty-eight women who signed the Declaration of Principles in 1848, only one lived to cast a ballot in 1920.[33]

The Seneca Falls Convention can be considered the beginning of the organized women's suffrage movement in the United States. It was not, however, the first women's movement. Since the founding of the republic under the Constitution of 1787, many women had joined the struggle to obtain other rights, such as the right to an education, the right to manage their own property after marriage, and the right to have custody of and guardianship over their children in the event of a divorce.

Married women had few rights in any of the states. If they worked outside the home, they did not have the right to control their own earnings. The husband had the right of guardianship over children. Property earned or acquired during the marriage by the wife was controlled by the husband. It could be disposed of in any way he wished—sold, given, or gambled away.[34]

Few women had the opportunity to obtain an education. Because society believed women to be frail, frivolous, and less mentally capable than men, an education in academic subjects was considered neither socially appropriate nor within women's intellectual capabilities. Free public education did not exist at the beginning of the nineteenth century, and until well into that century most of the private schools that existed for women taught the social graces and household management skills. But not everyone shared the negative view of education for women; some (both women and men) believed that women were as intellectually capable as men. In 1819 Emma Willard petitioned the New York State Assembly for a charter for a women's school and for a financial subsidy to establish a "female seminary" for young women. She received the charter but not the subsidy, and in 1821 she opened the Troy Female Seminary in Troy, New

York. However, even when schools for girls were established, the general lack of public funding for girls' education meant that education was available only to those whose families could afford to pay tuition at private schools. Public elementary schools for girls began to open in the 1820s. In 1824 the first public high school for girls opened in Worcester, Massachusetts, but free public high school education did not become available for girls, even in the larger cities, until after the Civil War.[35]

At the beginning of the nineteenth century men's colleges had existed for more than one hundred years, but a college education was not available to women. When Oberlin College opened in 1833 it admitted women, but initially not to the regular course of study. Not until 1841 did a woman who had completed the full course of study available to men graduate from Oberlin.[36]

The efforts to establish women's rights focused on many different issues, but leaders of the women's suffrage movement believed that gaining the right to vote was the key to obtaining other rights more quickly, because by targeting their votes, women might pressure legislators and executives to gain other rights.

The organized effort for women's suffrage lasted from 1848 to 1920. Progress was slow, in part because dissension fragmented the women's suffrage movement into competing and contentious organizations. Women's rights meetings were held both locally and nationally. National women's rights conventions were held almost every year between 1850 and 1860. At these meetings, women voiced their dissatisfaction with their lack of rights; such discussions helped them clarify their beliefs about preferable solutions. The press eventually began to treat the meetings seriously with factual reporting but little editorial support. Dissatisfied with the coverage, some women founded and edited journals that included both factual information about women's issues and sympathetic views.

The absence of a permanent organization handicapped the women's movement in its early years. Women also lacked the strategic weapons they needed to increase support for their cause. All the major institutions of society—state and national legislatures, the courts, the political parties, the press, religious organizations—were arrayed against the women's movement.

One strategy that leaders of the women's movement did use with some effectiveness was to petition state legislatures for specific changes in laws. The goals of Susan B. Anthony's efforts to change New York state laws were to obtain for women: (1) the right to control their own earnings;

(2) the right to obtain guardianship over their children in the event of divorce; and (3) the right to vote. Her petition drive led to the establishment of county-level and, later, state-level women's organizations.[37]

Leaders of the women's suffrage movement expected that the granting of political and legal rights to blacks after the Civil War would be accompanied by the extension of those rights to women. However, Republican congressional leaders, fearing that the constitutional amendments would not be ratified by the states if those rights were extended to women, restricted the applicability of the Fourteenth and Fifteenth Amendments to black males. Greatly disappointed that those amendments did not enfranchise women, Elizabeth Cady Stanton and Susan B. Anthony in 1869 established the National Woman Suffrage Association. The organization's goals were to obtain economic, social, political, and legal rights for women; one specific goal was the enactment of a constitutional amendment to enfranchise women. Believing that these goals were too broad and the strategy inappropriate, Lucy Stone in that year founded the American Woman Suffrage Association, which focused on the right to vote as the key to obtaining other policy changes, on the assumption that controversies associated with other goals could thus be avoided. The association also focused on obtaining the vote by means of state constitutional amendments rather than by a national constitutional amendment. These differences in goals and strategies divided the two organizations until 1890, when they merged to form the National American Woman Suffrage Association.

Several different interest groups opposed voting rights for women. Southern political leaders resented northern women's support for the abolitionist movement before and during the Civil War. The patriarchal culture that prevailed among southern political and social elites also contributed to southern opposition to women's political and legal rights. Conservative religious leaders in both the Catholic Church and fundamentalist Protestant churches opposed women's suffrage. Some business interests were afraid that women's support for laws prohibiting children from working in factories would be more effective if women had the vote. Opposition also came from leaders of the corrupt political organizations that controlled some city and state governments. These groups believed that women would support political reforms to reduce the power of political bosses and would thus bring about more honest government and politics. Women's activism and leadership in the temperance movement caused brewery and liquor interests to fear that women's enfranchisement would result in the success of that movement. When Congress finally proposed the Nineteenth Amendment in June

1919 and sent it to the states for ratification, many changes opposed by these interests had already become law. Many states had enacted laws prohibiting children from working in the mines and factories and had instituted political reforms that restricted the power of political bosses. In January 1919, a constitutional amendment had been ratified that prohibited the manufacture, sale, and transportation of alcoholic beverages. Indeed, the suffrage movement received support from representatives of interests that believed women would support their goals with their votes.

Largely as a result of the skillful leadership of such women as Carrie Chapman Catt, who became president of the National American Woman Suffrage Association in 1915, both Democratic and Republican Parties included planks supporting (although with a weak commitment) women's suffrage in their platforms in 1916. Catt sought to win the support of President Woodrow Wilson for women's suffrage. The association's leaders strengthened both its state and its national organizations in pursuit of their goal—enactment of the women's suffrage amendment by Congress and ratification by the states. One wing of the movement emphasized a continuing campaign to inform and persuade political decision makers. Another organized silent picketing movements, protest marches, and other demonstrations to keep the issue before the American people and their political leaders. President Wilson endorsed the Nineteenth Amendment in January 1918, and it passed in the House of Representatives by a vote of 274 to 136. However, the Senate did not approve the amendment during that term of Congress; it lost by one vote. Not until 1919 did both the Senate and the House of Representatives vote in favor of the amendment. A spirited drive for ratification in the states followed, and Tennessee became the thirty-sixth state to ratify the amendment on August 18, 1920.

Women in every state were now constitutionally guaranteed the right to vote. The campaign that had been sustained by the efforts of thousands of women in every state to educate and persuade and to organize support for women's right to vote had finally achieved its goal. The Nineteenth Amendment to the U.S. Constitution states:

> The right of citizens of the United States to vote shall not be denied or abridged by the United States or by any State on account of sex. Congress shall have the power to enforce this article by appropriate legislation.

The enactment of the Nineteenth Amendment was the beginning of a new chapter in the story of women's political participation. Since that time there have been radical changes in the way American women live their lives, as evidenced by Tomec and her daughters. The organized women's movement continues to challenge institutions and practices that prevent women from fully participating in all aspects of society, including politics. A major issue of the contemporary women's movement, for example, is women's reproductive freedom. Following in the tradition of Margaret Sanger and her efforts in the early part of the twentieth century, groups such as the National Association for Women (NOW) and NARAL Pro-Choice America (formerly the National Abortion and Reproductive Rights Action League) contend that control of a woman's reproductive life is essential if women are to take advantage of the hard-fought gains of the earlier women's movements. Not immune from change, the women's movement has been criticized that its agenda has advanced the interests of white, middle-class women. As a result, a movement known as "third wave feminism" has emerged. Following the first wave fight for suffrage and the post–World War II second wave fight for legal and political equality, third wave feminism attracts young women who bring a global perspective to the women's movement. Sometimes identified as "postfeminism," third wave feminism evolved in the late 1980s and early 1990s as a way of integrating factors such as race, ethnicity, and sexual identity into feminist theory and practice.[38]

American families and gender role expectations have changed, and this has created more options for women. Chapter 2 explores the effects of these and other cultural changes on women's political socialization and examines how the changes in political socialization have affected women.

SUGGESTIONS FOR FURTHER READING

In Print

Boisnier, Alicia D. 2003. "Race and Women's Identity Development: Distinguishing Between Feminism and Womanism Among Black and White Women." *Sex Roles* 49 (September): 211–218.
Bolks, Sean M., Diana Evans, J. L. Polinard, and Robert D. Wrinkle. 2000. "Core Beliefs and Abortion Attitudes: A Look at Latinos." *Social Science Quarterly* 81 (March): 253–260.

DePaz, Teresa Langle. 2002. "Beyond the Canon: New Documents on the Feminist Debate in Early Spain." *Hispanic Review* 70 (summer): 393–420.

Giddings, Paula. 1984. *When and Where I Enter: The Impact of Black Women on Race and Sex in America.* New York: Bantam Books.

McHenry, Robert. 2003. *Famous American Women: A Biographical Dictionary from Colonial Times to the Present.* New York: Dover Publications.

Perez, Beverly Encarguez. 2003. "Woman Warrior Meets Mail-Order Bride: Finding an Asian American Voice in the Women's Movement." *Berkeley Women's Law Journal* 18: 211–236.

Rundle, Lisa. 2003. "Marshalling in the Third Wave." *Horizons* 16 (spring): 15.

Waters, Anne. 2003. "Introduction: Special Issue on 'Native American Women, Feminism, and Indigenism.' " *Hypatia* 18 (spring): ix–xx.

Weisber, Herbert F., and Clyde Wilcox. 2004. *Models of Voting in Presidential Elections: The 2000 U.S. Election.* Stanford, Calif.: Stanford Law and Politics.

Wolbrecht, Christina. 2002. "Explaining Women's Rights Realignment: Convention Delegates, 1972–1992." *Political Behavior* 24 (September): 237–282.

On the Web

Black American Feminism. *www.library.ucsb.edu/blackfeminism.* Sherri L. Barnes at the University of California at Santa Barbara has compiled a bibliography of black feminist writings.

NARAL Pro-Choice America. *www.naral.org.* This site contains up-to-date information on reproductive issues and planned political actions.

National Organization for Women. *www.now.org.* The NOW Web site contains up-to-date material on women's issues and planned political actions.

Schooling, Education, and Literacy in Colonial America. *http://alumni.cc. gettysburg.edu/~s330558/schooling.html.* This Web site contains information about school materials and curriculum in colonial America, including pictures and details concerning the early schooling of girls.

NOTES

1. Eleanora Tomec was the mother of one of this book's coauthors.

2. Sara E. Rix, ed., for the Women's Research and Education Institute of the Congressional Caucus for Women's Issues, *The American Woman 1987–88: A Report in Depth* (New York: Norton, 1987), 292.

3. The divorce rate in 1945 was 3.5 divorces per 1,000 people. The marriage rate that year was 12.1 marriages per 1,000 people. U.S. Dept. of Commerce, Bureau of the Census, *Statistical Abstract of the United States, 1948* (Washington, D.C.: 1948), 89.

4. Ibid., 66.

5. Rix, *American Woman,* 302.

6. U.S. Dept. of Commerce, Bureau of the Census, *Statistical Abstract of the United States, 1948,* 169.

7. Paula Ries and Anne J. Stone, eds., for the Women's Research and Education Institute of the Congressional Caucus for Women's Issues, *The American Woman 1992–93: A Status Report* (New York: Norton, 1992), 236.

8. Herbert M. Levine, *Political Issues Debate: An Introduction to Politics,* 4th ed. (Englewood Cliffs, N.J.: Prentice-Hall, 1993), 20.

9. This is the focus used in M. Margaret Conway, David Ahern, and Gertrude A. Steuernagel, *Women and Public Policy: A Revolution in Progress* (Washington, D.C.: CQ Press, 1994). See particularly the discussion of women, public policy, and culture in chapter 1.

10. See, for example, John Rawls's widely acclaimed *A Theory of Justice* (Cambridge: Harvard University Press, 1971). According to a popular meaning of "liberal" today (not to be confused with the meaning used here), liberals are identified as supporters of big spending and big government but as opponents of family values.

11. M. Margaret Conway, *Political Participation in the United States,* 2d ed. (Washington, D.C.: CQ Press, 1991), 3–4.

12. Clearly, neither liberalism nor liberal culture is monolithic. There are groups that choose to live apart from the liberal culture (such as the Amish) and groups that, historically, have been denied the right to participate fully. Some observers have taken issue with the characterization of American culture as liberal. See, in particular, Richard M. Merelman, *Making Something of Ourselves: Our Culture and Politics in the United States* (Berkeley: University of California Press, 1984).

13. U.S. Dept. of Commerce, Bureau of the Census, *Statistical Abstract of the United States, 2002* (Washington, D.C.: 2003), 373.

14. Ries and Stone, *American Woman,* 308, 321.

15. U.S. Dept. of Commerce, Bureau of the Census, *Women and Men in the United States: March 2002* (Washington, D.C.: 2002), 3.

16. U.S. Dept. of Commerce, Bureau of the Census, *Statistical Abstract of the United States, 1948,* 169; *Statistical Abstract of the United States, 2002,* 382.

17. U.S. Dept. of Commerce, Bureau of the Census, *Statistical Abstract of the United States, 2002,* 381.

18. U.S. Dept. of Commerce, Bureau of the Census, *Statistical Abstract of the United States, 1951* (Washington, D.C.: 1951), 110.

19. U.S. Department of Commerce, Bureau of the Census, *Statistical Abstract of the United States, 2002,* 134, 139, 177.

20. See, for example, Theda Skocpol, *Protecting Soldiers and Mothers: The Political Origins of Social Policy in the United States* (Cambridge: Harvard University Press, Belknap Press, 1992).

21. Common law refers to that body of law arising from judicial decisions. This form of law developed before legislatures existed. It is contrasted with statutory law, which refers to laws enacted by legislatures. See Judith A. Baer, *Women in American Law* (New York: Holmes and Meier, 1991), 14–15.

22. Earlean McCarrick, "Women and Family Law: Marriage and Divorce," in Conway, Ahern, and Steuernagel, *Women and Public Policy,* 125–126.

23. Eleanor Flexner, *Century of Struggle,* rev. ed. (Cambridge: Harvard University Press, Belknap Press, 1975), 15.

24. Ibid.

25. Ibid., 167.

26. Ibid., 179; Conway, *Political Participation,* 13–15; John J. Stucker, "Women as Voters: Their Maturation as Political Persons in American Society," in Marianne Githens and Jewel L. Prestage, eds., *A Portrait of Marginality* (New York: McKay, 1977), Table 15.1, 267.

27. Stucker, "Women as Voters," Table 15.1, 267.

28. Ibid., Table 15.2, 269.

29. M. Margaret Conway, "Fostering Group-Based Political Participation," in Orit Ichilov, ed., *Political Socialization, Citizenship Education, and Democracy* (New York: Teacher's College Press, Columbia University, 1990), 297–312; Carole J. Uhlaner, "Rational Turnout: The Neglected Role of Groups," *American Journal of Political Science* 33 (1989): 390–422; Carole J. Uhlaner, " 'Relational Goods' and Participation: Incorporating Sociability into a Theory of Rational Action," *Public Choice* 62 (1988): 253–285.

30. Flexner, *Century of Struggle,* 73–74.

31. Elizabeth Cady Stanton, Susan B. Anthony, and Mathilda Joselyn Gage, eds., *The History of Woman Suffrage,* vol. 1 (Rochester, N.Y.: Susan B. Anthony and Charles Mann, 1881–1922), 72.

32. Upon hearing the draft resolution concerning the vote, Stanton's husband informed Stanton that he would leave town if that resolution were introduced at the convention. Flexner, *Century of Struggle,* 75.

33. Ibid., 77.

34. McCarrick, "Women and Family Law"; Dorothy McBride Stetson, *Women's Rights in the U.S.A.* (Pacific Grove, Calif.: Brooks/Cole, 1991), 138.

35. Flexner, *Century of Struggle,* 25–28.

36. Ibid., 29–30.

37. Ibid., 86. The remainder of this discussion draws on chapters 10, 22, and 23 of Flexner.

38. For a fuller discussion of these points, see Amanda D. Lotz, "Communicating Third-Wave Feminism and New Social Movements: Challenges for the Next Century of Feminist Endeavor," *Women and Language* 26 (2003): 2–9.

CHAPTER 2

Women, Culture, and Political Socialization

Barbara Jordan was born in the segregated city of Houston, Texas, in 1936. From the beginning, family and friends recognized her abilities and urged her to set her sights beyond Houston.[1] Because she was the daughter of a minister, church and family were the foundations of her life. Because her skin was dark and she did not have "good hair," Jordan experienced discrimination on the part of some blacks, including teachers. Having watched her mother toil to provide for her family, Jordan knew she did not want to spend her life scrubbing floors, cooking, and washing clothes. She always knew she would go to college, and at some point during high school she decided to become a lawyer. Her matriculation at Boston University Law School marked her entry, for the first time, into the white world, where people frequently treated her as a black woman rather than as an individual. But Jordan learned to cope. She and other black students started their own study group when they were not invited to join any of the white study groups. She endured "Ladies Day," when she and the other usually ignored women in the law school class were actually called upon to participate. Jordan worked long hours; her segregated education had not adequately prepared her for the demands of law school. Her family supported her both emotionally and financially, and she received her law degree in 1959. She returned to Houston, established a law practice, and became involved in John F. Kennedy's campaign for the presidency. "Bitten by the bug" of politics, she soon gained attention as a speaker at liberal Democratic gatherings.

Jordan found politics attractive in part because it was a way to do something to implement school desegregation. Houston had all but ignored the Supreme Court's ruling in *Brown v. Board of Education* (1954), and in 1962 the U.S. Court of Appeals, in *Ross v. Dyer,* ruled that the Houston school system was discriminating against black students.[2] The *Ross* case was a catalyst for Jordan's entry into politics. She developed some connections, and in 1962 entered her first race for a seat in the Texas House of Representatives. But she lost that race, as well as her 1964 bid for the same office. It was at this point that Jordan, who had always been ambivalent about marriage because it might confine her choices, decided that she could not have both marriage and a career in politics. She realized that public expectations were different for her as a black woman than they were for a white man. A man was perceived as capable of combining marriage with a career in politics because his wife would take care of the domestic responsibilities. If she, as a black woman, were to defy expectations, she would have to make a choice; she chose politics over marriage. It was at this time that President Kennedy was assassinated, Lyndon Baines Johnson succeeded him, the Civil Rights Act of 1964 was passed, and the U.S. Supreme Court issued a series of reapportionment decisions.[3] Texas, like the rest of the country, was changing.

In 1966 Barbara Jordan ran for a state senate seat and became the first black woman in the Texas legislature. She was aware that her race and gender might make some of her new colleagues uncomfortable, and she did her best to fit in. She made it clear, for example, that although she did not use profane language, she would not object if others used it in her presence. In 1968 she was reelected to the Texas senate, and in 1972 she won a seat in the U.S. House of Representatives, securing a coveted spot on the Judiciary Committee. In 1974, when that committee began hearings on the impeachment of President Richard Nixon, her opening statement thrust her into the national spotlight. Her articulate keynote address at the 1976 Democratic National Convention further enhanced her reputation.

Jordan's supporters had hoped that Jimmy Carter would ask her to be his running mate. When he did not, discussion centered on a cabinet post for her. From Jordan's perspective, it would have to be attorney general or nothing. But again she was passed over, and in 1976 voters reelected her to Congress.[4]

Jordan began to tire of the House and to think about leaving politics. Eventually she decided not to seek a fourth term. She then devoted herself to teaching and nonelected public service. In 1994 Barbara Jordan won the Presidential Medal of Freedom. She died in Texas in 1996. President Bill Clinton spoke at her funeral.

CULTURAL CHANGE AND GENDER ROLE EXPECTATIONS

A useful way to organize our thinking about the cultural changes that Barbara Jordan and other women have experienced is to analyze the "social clock"—a term that psychologists define as society's expectations, including those for gender roles, concerning appropriate behavior at different ages in life. All members of society are aware of these implicit expectations, for society supports those who conform to this timetable and criticizes those who do not.[5] In 1950 a mother who worked outside the home when her children were very young would be contradicting the social clock. But should she decide to stay home and out of the paid work force until her youngest child graduated from high school, she would win approval. If Barbara Jordan had been a man, her life would have been a model of compliance with the social clock. Her elementary and high school years were notable because of her many accolades and achievements. She went to college following high school and entered law school immediately after college. Jordan then began to build what would be a successful career in law and politics.

Had she been a man, Jordan would still have been expected to marry and father children. In this respect she would not have conformed with the social clock; but because marriage and family were not considered as central to a man's existence as they were to a woman's, the disapproval might have been less severe than it was for Jordan. As a woman of color, however, Jordan was expected to marry and have children and to make these the primary focus of her life. If she wanted a career (one that she would be expected to willingly interrupt during her children's younger years), the expectation was that she would choose between education and social work. But Jordan chose politics, and in doing so she risked disapproval and ultimately incurred much of the negativity that accompanies nonconformance with the social clock. In this case, however, her rebellion came at a time when the culture was changing. The 1960s saw tremendous social upheaval that gave rise to a number of movements for change, including the women's movement. For the individual willing to risk disapproval, as was Barbara Jordan, the opportunities were there. This change in the social clock is evident in the contrast between the life of Eleanora Tomec and the lives of her daughters.

Eleanora Tomec's life also reflected some contradictions of the social clock, but none were as radical as Barbara Jordan's. Tomec delayed marriage and childbearing, but because World War II was a contributing factor, Tomec did not receive the strong disapproval that would have been predicted by the social clock of her time. Another contradiction was that she went back to work while her children were small. But she returned to an appropriate profession, that of secretary, and she always placed her family's interests ahead of her work. She also worked to finance her children's education—a justification for women's work that was more acceptable at the time than reasons such as advancement of her own career or the desire to achieve something for herself. According to the social clock, Tomec's daughters were expected to pursue college educations, and they did. Although the younger daughter married relatively late in life, she was part of a continuing trend for professional women. The older daughter's divorce was not met with the disapproval that Tomec might have experienced at the same age, for society now accepts divorce. The younger daughter's decision to remain in the work force during her child's preschool years was also not something that, according to the social clock of her time, would engender disapproval. Tomec, her daughters, and Barbara Jordan lived with an awareness of the social clocks of their time, and in living their lives they helped to change gender role expectations.

GENDER ROLE EXPECTATIONS AND POLITICAL SOCIALIZATION

Why did Barbara Jordan become a political activist? In what ways and to what extent did her family, church, schools, the Democratic Party, and the American culture as a whole shape her political attitudes? Such questions are the focus of the field of study known as political socialization. This field studies political learning, which, like any kind of learning, continues throughout a person's life. Political socialization is the process by which people learn what is expected of them in their particular political system.[6]

Women's political socialization should be understood in the context of cultural expectations for gender roles. Despite the many changes in gender roles, men and women continue to face different expectations, and these translate into differences in political participation.

As girls, women learn to be more passive than boys and to care about things not commonly thought of as political. Furthermore, the socialization women experience as adults, in their family roles, has been thought to reinforce the idea that politics is not their business. Women have for so long been culturally restricted to the private world of home and family that when they enter the public world of politics, they face a struggle to be viewed as public figures, not private individuals.[7] Women's family responsibilities have been found to affect their political ambition and the kinds of political activism they pursue.[8] As the tie between women and the private world of home and family lessens, politics is increasingly viewed as an appropriate area in which women can participate. Traditionally, women have not developed the sense of political efficacy—the sense that what a person does really matters—that is usually associated with political partic-ipation. Women (as well as men) did not accept the idea that politics should be of concern to women. They did not run for political office because it was not considered "right," and party leaders and voters agreed. Women also had more domestic responsibilities, which constrained the time they had to devote to politics. Even among political activists, women were more likely than men to curtail their political involvement to make time for family. When women did become involved in politics, their activity was likely to be related to their roles in the family, centering on local issues such as education.[9]

Cultural change has clearly had a direct impact on women's political participation. In general, changes in gender role expectations have both reflected and given rise to changes in gender role socialization. These changes, in turn, affect how women perceive politics. Patterns of political participation change with life experiences, and cultural change in women's roles is required for women to become completely integrated into the world of politics.[10] Although women now vote in proportions equal to or greater than men, gender differences in political attitudes and other voting behavior remain. Women, for example, are less likely than men to be inter-ested in politics or to engage in political discussions.[11] Overall, young men seem to be more politicized—that is, they have more of an awareness of politics and more motivation to participate—than young women.[12] Cultural change has made politics less a "man's thing," but differences in the way women and men live their lives continue to affect women's political behavior.

But the barriers to women's full participation in the nation's political affairs are not all attitudinal. Situational factors, such as the demands of family life, and structural factors, such as lack of education, experience, and money, can limit a woman's ability to be politically active.[13] Women are still less likely than men to be members of the legal profession, a career that is compatible with a career in politics (as in the case of Barbara Jordan). As more women enter the legal profession, more are likely to pursue leadership roles in politics. Cultural change has lessened the impact of situational and structural factors on women's political participation, but women's full participation in political affairs will occur only when men and women have the same degree of access to educational and employment opportunities. Research suggests, for example, that women's level of political engagement, including discussing politics and attempting to influence others politically, increases when a competitive female candidate is running in an election.[14]

CULTURAL CHANGE AND THE AGENTS OF SOCIALIZATION

Cultural change and political socialization are closely related.[15] Students of political socialization have always been concerned with agents of socialization such as family, school, workplace, church, peer group, and the media.[16] The tremendous cultural changes that occurred in the twentieth century have shaped all of these agents and have also affected women's political socialization.

Family

The family, traditionally thought of as the primary agent of political socialization, is where children learn political attitudes and a basic orientation toward politics, particularly party identification. Attitudes toward both traditional and nontraditional forms of political activism are also thought to be transmitted in the family. Party activist parents, for example, are more likely to have children who become involved in party politics. Children of parents who were involved in political protests also seem to "inherit" their parents' inclination and are more likely to participate in such protests.[17]

Even the media as an agent of political socialization may well have made its first impact on a person in the context of the family. A child, for example, may begin to watch television news with a parent.[18] The impact of cultural change on the family has been dramatic; gender role expectations have changed as women's roles in the family have changed. Polling data reveal that by the end of the 1980s a majority of married women and men in the United States believed that the arrangement that worked best for them was one in which both spouses worked outside the home and shared domestic and child-rearing responsibilities. But as recently as the mid-1970s, a majority of both women and men wanted a marriage in which the husband was the financial provider and the wife cared for the children and the home.[19]

Marriage and family continue to be part of most women's lives, but women are now marrying later in life than women did in the 1970s. In 1970 the median age for women at the time of first marriage was 20.8 years. By 2002 this figure had increased to 25.3 years. Women are having fewer children than did women in the 1970s. They are also more likely than women were in the 1970s to be divorced and to be single parents.[20] In 1970, 11.9 percent of children under the age of eighteen lived with a single parent. By 2002, 23 percent of all children lived with only their mothers; and this varies for children of certain racial and ethnic groups. In 2002, for example, 16 percent of white, non-Hispanic children lived with single mothers compared with 48 percent of black children and 25 percent of Hispanic children.[21] Mothers and fathers alike are now coping with the demands of family and work, and young children are frequently cared for by people other than Mommy or Daddy.

School

In general, education and political knowledge, whether it comes from formal schooling or other sources such as life experiences, are linked to higher levels of political participation. Education also impacts political attitudes. Mexican Americans, for example, are more likely than Mexicans in Mexico to favor opposition political parties. Higher levels of education among Mexican Americans explains most of this difference.[22] During the twentieth century, American women became more and more educated, and the trend continues. Women in the twenty-first century are more likely to be high school graduates than were women in the 1970s. They are also more likely to be enrolled in college; at all levels except the doctorate, there are more female than male degree recipients. This is not to say, however, that there has been a total change in gender role expectations. Although women are becoming more educated, they still tend to choose fields whose occupations are extensions of traditionally female roles such as early childhood education and nursing. They are less likely than men to major in such disciplines as computer science and engineering.[23]

Workplace

Women now constitute a greater proportion of the labor force than they did in 1970. Indeed, women's membership in the work force has steadily increased since the 1960s; more than half of all employed women are now full-time, year-round workers. Employment outside the home is now the norm for all women, although black women (62.9 percent) are more likely than white (59.7 percent) or Hispanic (56.8 percent) women to work outside the home. Even women with less than a high school education are now more likely (50.4 percent) to be employed than not. Eighty-two percent of women with college degrees work outside the home. As late as 1970, only 40.5 percent of married women had jobs outside the home. By 2000 this had increased to 61.3 percent. The trend is particularly dramatic in the case of women with young children. Over 62 percent of married women with children under the age of six and 70.5 percent of single women with children under the age of six are employed outside the home.[24]

In general, although more women are now working outside the home, women's choice of fields and occupations has not changed much. Although women are moving into traditionally male fields such as medicine and law, there are still few women employed in skilled construction trades. Overall, women are concentrated in a narrower range of occupations than men; and these occupations, like women's choice of fields of study, tend to reflect traditional gender role expectations.[25]

Implications of Cultural Change in Agents of Political Socialization

Changes in the agents of political socialization affect the direction of future changes in women's political participation. As more women become more educated, they are more likely to be interested in and to participate in politics and to have a greater sense of their own political efficacy.[26] There is some evidence suggesting that in general, women who work outside the home have higher levels of political participation than women who are homemakers. Research also suggests that homemakers are less egalitarian in their beliefs than women in the work force. Moreover, women in the work force are more likely to try to persuade others how to vote, to attend political rallies, and to make campaign contributions.[27]

Adult socialization can occur in the workplace. This is significant because women continue to move into the labor force in unprecedented numbers. Socialization involves adapting to the environment, and this adaptation involves changes in attitudes.[28] (It is difficult to determine the exact nature of the process, however, because some self-selection takes place; women who enter the work force may be inherently different from those who do not—for example, they may be more self-confident.) Evangelical women are a case in point. Evangelical women in the work force have more egalitarian attitudes concerning the role of women in politics and business than do evangelical homemakers, although both groups continue to hold traditional beliefs about their own roles as wives and mothers.[29]

These changes in life experience affect how women perceive themselves as women. Some women continue to define themselves in terms of traditional roles. Interestingly, women and men who continue to hold traditional views regarding women and politics are less likely to vote, less likely to be active in political campaigns and organizations concerned with national problems, and less likely to be politically active than those with more modern ideas.[30] It is also possible that women who experience the impact of these cultural changes, including changes in the traditional roles, will begin to see themselves not as isolated individuals but as members of a group with shared concerns. Gender consciousness, defined as "the recognition that one's relation to the political world is shaped in important ways by the physical fact of one's sex,"[31] will not lead all women to adopt the same political position, but it is necessary if women, who were once denied the opportunity of political participation because of their gender, are to understand that being female has political significance and to act accordingly.

Not all women with gender consciousness support the women's movement, for example, but without gender consciousness women will not perceive themselves as a group with shared political interests. What is clear is that women's political participation increases as women's consciousness of themselves as a group increases.[32] The women's movement has contributed to the effort to help women develop gender consciousness. The National Organization for Women has successfully worked for the passage of legislation in such areas as credit, sexual harassment, and health care. Its members believe that the policies they support not only improve women's lives but also help to empower women by making them more aware of the experiences and needs they share as women—an important step in the development of gender consciousness among women.[33]

Not all women share the same experiences, however, and this can affect the development of gender consciousness. For some women, race or religion may be more important politically than gender; for others, their economic situation may be the factor that is most politically relevant.[34] Economically, women are clearly not a monolithic group. In 2002, for example, 10.4 percent of all families lived below poverty level. In comparison, 28.8 percent of all families headed by women with no husband present lived in poverty. Again, looking at 2002, 8.4 percent of all white families and 24.1 percent of all white female-headed families lived in poverty. Poverty is more prevalent among black families, 22.8 percent of whom lived in poverty in 2002. For black families headed by women the figure increased to 38.2 percent. The same is true for Hispanics. In 2002, 20.8 percent of Hispanic families and 36.4 percent of female-headed (and no husband present) families lived below the poverty line. Although Asian families are less likely than white, black, or Hispanic families to live in poverty, Asian families headed by women with no husband present are more likely than Asian families in general to live below the poverty line.[35] In general, women earn less than men, but the picture is complicated by such factors as race and ethnic origin.

Overall, men have more years of work experience and work more hours than women. Women, in contrast, are more likely than men to work less than full-time and to take longer periods of time off from work. Even these factors, however, cannot explain all the differences in wages between men and women.[36] Discrimination may explain some of the wage gap, and even this answer begs the question as to why it is women and not men who have work patterns that place family and personal responsibilities first. White men earn more than white women; black men earn more than black women; Asian men earn more than Asian women; and Hispanic men earn more than Hispanic women. In 2002 Asian women had a higher median income ($17,313) than white ($16,216), black ($16,084), or Hispanic ($12,249) women, but this was lower than the median income for the lowest earning group of men, Hispanics ($19,829).[37]

Age also affects the development of gender consciousness. The period in which a woman is born and her age at the time of significant societal change tend to shape her political beliefs.[38] Baby boomers—people born between 1946 and 1964—are the group commonly thought to be most affected by the women's movement and by public policies such as Title IX of the Higher Education Act Amendments (which prohibited sexual discrimination by educational institutions). But there are generational differences even among baby boomers. A girl born in 1946 would have been twenty-six years old at the time of the enactment of Title IX. A girl born in 1964 would have been eight years old—young enough to avail herself of the opportunities afforded by Title IX but also too young to appreciate that women had not always had such opportunities. Nonetheless, there is evidence that young women recognize the benefits of policies such as Title IX. In 1999 the twenty American women who won the World Cup in soccer called themselves the "Title IX Team."[39] Moreover, lesbians and gay men acknowledge the protections Title IX affords them from bias based on real or perceived sexual orientation.[40] In addition, between 1971 and 2000 there was a 955 percent increase in the National Collegiate Athletic Association (NCAA) sports participation by female college athletes of color and, at the same time, participation opportunities for male athletes of color did not decrease.[41]

There is some indication that support for feminism will increase among women as more of them experience the impact of changes in the traditional roles of wife and mother.[42] It is also possible that women will increasingly identify psychologically with one another even though they differ in terms of class, race, and age.[43] As women continue to share experiences at home, school, and work, these psychological bonds may contribute to the development of gender consciousness.

IT'S A MAN'S WORLD,
BUT TIMES ARE CHANGING

In analyzing the consequences of cultural change for agents of political socialization as they affect both women and political participation, it is helpful to think of women's increased political involvement in terms of acculturation, the process by which one group becomes integrated into the way of life of another group. Immigrants have traditionally become acculturated to the way of living of their adopted homeland, but acculturation can take a variety of forms. As discussed in Chapter 1, Eleanora Tomec's parents wanted her to be an American. For them, this meant that Tomec was to speak, dress, and conduct herself as an American. Their own acculturation was less complete. They learned to speak English, but they frequently spoke their native Slovenian to each other. Although Tomec's mother continued to cook and bake Slovenian dishes, she never taught her daughter how to prepare them but rather insisted that because American men liked American food, Tomec should learn how to prepare hamburgers and hot dogs. What Tomec's parents seemed not to understand was that acculturation, particularly in the United States, is seldom linear. Immigrants have reshaped American culture in the process of joining it. Tomec's mother's strudel is therefore as American as apple pie.

As women become more involved in politics, they become more acculturated. Given the history of male domination of political affairs in the United States, women's increased participation in politics is comparable to a wave of immigration. Barbara Jordan attempted to fit in with other members of the Texas state legislature. One indication of male domination of political affairs is the number of sports and military metaphors used in speaking and writing about politics. A campaign is a "run" for political office. The leading candidate is the front runner and an unknown is a dark horse. A pollster frequently uses a "horse race question." A candidate who is hurt by an opponent's attack may be "down for the count." The candidate who does not foresee an opponent's strategy may be "ambushed." Some candidates choose to run a "stealth" campaign and to "hunker down" or "stay in the bunkers" to avoid engagement with their opponents. This gives them time to "circle the wagons" and orchestrate a defense against the opponents' attacks. Election day volunteers involved in get-out-the-vote activities are known as "foot soldiers." Other volunteers may call upon "targets," or selected voters.

If women are to become fully integrated into politics, a certain amount of acculturation must occur; women need to think of themselves as public figures as well as private individuals. As increasing numbers of women participate politically, they are changing the culture of politics. One study found female state legislators to be more supportive than their male colleagues of conducting government business in public view rather than behind closed doors. The same study revealed that female state legislators were more likely than their male colleagues to bring citizens into the policy-making process.[44] Changes are also being observed in the political agenda. An issue such as child care is now considered an appropriate item for the political agenda rather than strictly a private matter. In addition, some candidates for political office, cognizant of the gender gap in voting, take care to promote themselves as the "environmental governor" or the "education president." Even Congress, one of the most traditional and most male-dominated political institutions, made its gymnasium facilities available to female members around 1985.[45]

Like the acculturation of immigrant groups, however, the political integration of women is affected by a number of factors, such as the perception of a woman's capabilities and qualifications. Much of what immigrants do in adapting to the political culture of their new country is a function of that country's attitudes toward them. In receptive host countries, immigrants are likely to attempt to unlearn their old political attitudes, a process known as desocialization, and to learn new ones that are appropriate to their new homeland, a process known as resocialization. When the host country is not particularly receptive, however, immigrants may adopt some of the new attitudes, but they usually do not desocialize or resocialize.[46] To a large extent, then, the future of women's political participation depends on the receptivity of what has been a male-oriented political culture.

SUGGESTIONS FOR FURTHER READING

In Print

Calvert, Sandra L., Amy B. Jordan, and Rodney R. Cocking, eds. 2002. *Children in the Digital Age: Influences of Electronic Media on Development.* Westport, Conn.: Praeger.

Campbell, David E. 2002. "The Youth and the Realigning: A Test of the Socialization Theory of Realignment." *Public Opinion Quarterly* 66: 209–234.

Collins, Patricia Hill. 1991. *Black Feminist Thought: Knowledge, Consciousness, and the Politics of Empowerment.* New York: Routledge.

Hritzuk, Natasha, and David K. Park. 2000. "The Question of Latino Participation: From an SES to a Social Structural Explanation." *Social Science Quarterly* 81, no. 1 (March): 151–166.

Jackson, David J. 2002. *Entertainment and Politics: The Influence of Pop Culture on Young Adult Political Socialization.* New York: P. Lang.

Lien, Pei-te, M. Margaret Conway, and Janelle Wong. 2003. "The Contours and Sources of Ethnic Identity Choices Among Asian Americans." *Social Science Quarterly* 84, no. 2 (June): 461–481.

McDevitt, Michael, and Steven Chaffee. 2002. "From Top Down to Trickle-Up Influence: Revisiting Assumptions About the Family in Political Socialization." *Political Communication* 19: 281–301.

Patrick, John J. 2002. "Political Socialization of Youth: Reconsideration of Research on the Civic Development of Elementary and Secondary School Students in the United States and Abroad." *The International Social Studies Forum* 2, no. 1: 59–65.

Roots, James. 1999. *The Politics of Visual Language: Deafness, Language Choice, and Political Socialization.* Ottawa: Carleton University Press.

Young, Iris Marion. 1994. "Gender as Seriality: Thinking about Women as a Social Collective." *Signs* 19, no. 3 (spring): 713–738. ˙

On the Web

About-Face. *www.about-face.org.* This site analyzes and satirizes negative images of women in society.

Association for Women in Sport's Media. *www.awsmonline.org.* This site contains information for women interested in a sport's media career, including information on conventions and scholarship.

Girls, Women + Media Project. *www.mediaandwomen.org.* This site aims to increase awareness of girls and women in the media.

League of Women Voters. *www.lwv.org.* This site supports informed political participation and has information on current political issues.

National Coalition for Women and Girls in Education. *www.ncwge.org.* This group advocates for educational opportunities for women and girls. It has a great deal of information on educational policy issues, including federal legislation.

NOTES

1. All of the information concerning Barbara Jordan is from Barbara Jordan and Shelby Hearon, *Barbara Jordan: A Self-Portrait* (Garden City, N.Y.: Doubleday, 1979).

2. *Brown v. Board of Education,* 347 U.S. 483 (1954); *Ross v. Dyer,* 312 F. 2d 191 (5th Cir. 1962).

3. *Baker v. Carr,* 369 U.S. 186 (1962); *Reynolds v. Sims,* 377 U.S. 533 (1963); *Wesberry v. Sanders,* 376 U.S. 1 (1964).

4. Not until the election of President Bill Clinton in 1992 would there be a female attorney general—Janet Reno. When Clinton was reelected in 1996, one of his first appointments was Madeleine K. Albright, who was confirmed as the first female secretary of state. A woman has not yet held either of the two other major cabinet posts—secretary of defense and Treasury secretary.

5. Irene H. Frieze, Jacquelynne E. Parsons, Paula B. Johnson, Diane N. Ruble, and Gail L. Zellman, *Women and Sex Roles: A Social Psychological Perspective* (New York: Norton, 1978), 163–164.

6. For a general discussion of political socialization, including its "ups and downs," see Pamela Johnston Conover, "Political Socialization: Where's the Politics?" in William Crotty, ed., *Political Science: Looking to the Future*, vol. 3, *Political Behavior* (Evanston, Ill.: Northwestern University Press, 1991), 125–152.

7. Virginia Sapiro, *The Political Integration of Women: Roles, Socialization, and Politics* (Urbana: University of Illinois Press, 1983), chap. 2.

8. Virginia Sapiro and Barbara Farah, "New Pride and Old Prejudice: Political Ambition and Role Orientations among Female Partisan Elites," *Women and Politics* 1, no. 1 (spring 1980): 13–36.

9. For a discussion of women running for political office, see Susan J. Carroll, *Women as Candidates in American Politics,* 2d ed. (Bloomington: Indiana University Press, 1994), 310–323; and Virginia Sapiro, "Private Costs of Public Commitments or Public Costs of Private Commitments? Family Roles Versus Political Ambition," *American Journal of Political Science* 26, no. 2 (May 1982): 265–279.

10. Sapiro, *Political Integration of Women,* 27; M. Margaret Conway, *Political Participation in the United States,* 2d ed. (Washington, D.C.: CQ Press, 1991), 29.

11. Gertrude A. Steuernagel, Thom Yantek, and Irene Barnett, "More Than Pink and Blue: Gender, Occupational Stratification, and Political Attitudes," in Lois Lovelace Duke, ed., *Women in Politics: Outsiders or Insiders?* 2d ed. (Chicago: Prentice Hall, 1996).

12. Diana Owen and Jack Dennis, "Sex Differences in Politicization: The Influence of Mass Media," *Women and Politics* 12, no. 4 (1992): 19–41. See also Diana Owen and Jack Dennis, "Gender Differences in the Politicization of American Children," *Women and Politics* 8, no. 2 (1988): 23–43.

13. Much of the research, particularly the early work, on women and political participation has focused on the relative effects of socialization and situational and structural factors. See Cal Clark and Janet Clark, "Models of Gender and Political Participation in the United States," *Women and Politics* 6, no. 1 (spring 1986): 5–25; Susan C. Bourque and Jean Grossholtz, "Politics and Unnatural Practice: Political Science Looks at Female Participation," *Politics and Society* 2, no. 4 (1974): 225–266; Susan B. Hansen, Linda M. Franz, and Margaret Netemeyer-Mays, "Women's Political Participation and Policy Preferences," *Social Science Quarterly* 56, no. 4 (March 1976): 576–590; Fred I. Greenstein, "Sex-Related Political Differences in Childhood," *Journal of Politics* 23, no. 2 (May 1961): 353–371; Kent L. Tedin, David W. Brady, and Arnold Vedlitz, "Sex Differences in Political Attitudes: The Case for Situational Factors," *Journal of Politics* 39, no. 2 (May 1977): 448–456; Kristi Andersen, "Working Women and Political Participation: 1952–1972," *American Journal of Political Science* 19, no. 3 (August 1975): 439–453; Susan Welch, "Women as Political Animals? A Test of Some Explanations for Male-

Female Political Participation Differences," *American Journal of Political Science* 21, no. 4 (November 1977): 711–730; Anthony M. Orum, Roberta S. Cohen, Sherri Grasmuck, and Amy W. Orum, "Sex, Socialization, and Politics," *American Sociological Review* 39, no. 2 (April 1974): 197–209; Susan Gluck Mezey, "Does Sex Make a Difference? A Case Study of Women in Politics," *Western Political Quarterly* 31, no. 4 (December 1978): 493–501; Fred I. Greenstein, *Children and Politics* (New Haven: Yale University Press, 1969).

14. Lonna Rae Atkeson, "Not All Cues Are Created Equal: The Conditional Impact of Female Candidates on Political Engagement," *Journal of Politics* 65, no. 4 (November 2003): 1040–1061.

15. For a more detailed discussion of theories about women and political socialization, see Clark and Clark, "Gender and Political Participation," 5–25.

16. Those interested in comparative politics should see, for example, Michael H. Banks and Debra Roker, "The Political Socialization of Youth: Exploring the Influence of School Experience," *Journal of Adolescence* 17 (1994): 3–15, for a discussion of political socialization in England. Also useful is Anders Westholm and Richard G. Niemi, "Political Institutions and Political Socialization: A Cross-National Study," *Comparative Politics* 25, no. 1 (October 1992): 25–41.

17. Darren E. Sherkat and T. Jean Blocker, "The Political Development of the Sixties' Activists: Identifying the Influence of Class, Gender, and Socialization on Protest Participation," *Social Forces* 72, no. 3 (March 1994): 821–842.

18. Marco Calavita, "Within the Context of Many Contexts: Family, News Media Engagement, and the Ecology of Individual Political Development Among 'Generationa Xers,'" *The Communication Review* 6 (2003): 23–43.

19. Cited in Nancy E. McGlen and Karen O'Connor, *Women, Politics, and American Society* (Englewood Cliffs, N.J.: Prentice-Hall, 1995), 250.

20. Cynthia Costello and Anne J. Stone, eds., for the Women's Research and Education Institute of the Congressional Caucus for Women's Issues, *The American Woman 1994–95: Where We Stand* (New York: Norton, 1994), 256, 258, 259, 261.

21. Paula Ries and Anne J. Stone, eds., for the Women's Research and Education Institute of the Congressional Caucus for Women's Issues, *American Woman 1992–93: A Status Report* (New York: Norton, 1992), 256. Federal Interagency Forum on Child and Family Statistics, *America's Children 2003,* www.childstats.gov.

22. Chappell Lawson, "Voting Preference and Political Socialization among Mexican Americans and Mexicans Living in the United States," *Mexican Studies* 19, no. 1 (winter 2003): 66.

23. U.S. Department of Commerce, U.S. Bureau of the Census, *Statistical Abstract of the United States: 2002* (Washington, D.C.: 2002), 175–176.

24. Ibid., 367, 369, 372, 373, 381.

25. Ibid.

26. Carroll, *Women as Candidates,* 323.

27. Kristi Andersen and Elizabeth A. Cook, "Women, Work, and Political Attitudes," *American Journal of Political Science* 29, no. 3 (August 1985): 613.

28. Ibid., 606–625.

29. Clyde Wilcox, "Evangelicalism, Social Identity, and Gender Attitudes among Women," *American Politics Quarterly* 19, no. 3 (July 1991): 353–363.

30. Linda L. M. Bennett and Stephen E. Bennett, "Changing Views About Gender Equality in Politics: Gradual Change and Lingering Doubts," in Duke, *Women in Politics,* 46–66.

31. Sue Tolleson-Rinehart, *Gender Consciousness and Politics* (New York: Routledge, 1992), 14.

32. Arthur H. Miller, Patricia Gurin, Gerald Gurin, and Oksana Malanchuk, "Group Consciousness and Political Participation," *American Journal of Political Science* 25, no. 3 (August 1981): 494–511.

33. Ethel Klein, *Gender Politics* (Cambridge: Harvard University Press, 1984), 3.

34. Melanie McCoy, "Gender or Ethnicity: What Makes a Difference? A Study of Women Tribal Leaders," *Women and Politics* 12, no. 3 (1992): 57–68.

35. Seven percent of Asian families live below the poverty line; 15.2 percent of female-headed Asian families with no husband present live below the poverty line. U.S. Census Bureau, *Poverty in the United States: 2002* (Washington, D.C.: 2003): 22–26.

36. United States General Accounting Office, *Women's Earnings: Work Patterns Partially Explain Difference Between Men's and Women's Earnings* (Washington, D.C.: 2003).

37. U.S. Department of Commerce, U.S. Census Bureau, *Statistical Abstract of the United States: 2002,* 440.

38. Paul Allen Beck and M. Kent Jennings, "Family Traditions, Political Periods, and the Development of Partisan Orientations," *Journal of Politics* 53, no. 3 (August 1991): 743.

39. For more information on this point and for more details on other prominent women who have benefited from Title IX, see "Happy Birthday, Title IX," available on the Web site of CNN/SI at http://sportsillustrated.cnn.com/soccer/world/1999/womens_worldcup/news/1999/07/17/wwc-titleix/.

40. The enforcement of this aspect of Title IX is a "work in progress" rather than a finished product. For more details see "Homophobia Rampant in Women's Sports" at the Web site of Outsports at www.outsports.com/campus/titleixdekoven.htm.

41. For more information on this and to view the entire report, go to the Web site of the Women's Sports Foundation at www.womenssportsfoundation.org.

42. Klein, *Gender Politics,* 165. See also McGlen and O'Connor, *Women, Politics, and American Society,* 305.

43. Jeffrey W. Kock, "Is Group Membership a Prerequisite for Group Identification?" *Political Behavior* 15, no. 1 (March 1993): 49–60.

44. Susan J. Carroll, Debra L. Dodson, and Ruth B. Mandel, *The Impact of Women in Public Office: An Overview* (New Brunswick, N.J.: Center for the American Woman and Politics, Eagleton Institute of Politics, Rutgers University, 1991), 23.

45. Male-dominated political institutions do not readily change without a little help. Concerning the integration of the gymnasium of the House of Representatives, see Barbara Boxer and Nicole Boxer, *Strangers in the Senate: Politics and the New Revolution of Women in America* (Washington, D.C.: National Press Books, 1993), 109–112.

46. For a fuller discussion, see Marilyn Hoskin, "Socialization and Anti-Socialization: The Case of Immigrants," in Roberta S. Sigel, ed., *Political Learning in Adulthood: A Sourcebook of Theory and Research* (Chicago: University of Chicago Press, 1989), 340–377.

CHAPTER 3

Gender Differences in Political Attitudes, Beliefs, and Policy Preferences

Jim and Sue are happily married. They preserve their marital tranquility by not discussing political issues about which they strongly disagree. One such issue is gun control. Sue opposes individual ownership of handguns; Jim believes that every citizen should have the right to own as many guns of whatever type he or she wants. Such disagreements raise many questions: Do men and women differ in their policy preferences, perceptions of and support for candidates and political parties, and beliefs about the political system? Do women differ among themselves in their policy preferences? If so, to what extent? What are the possible explanations for gender differences in political orientation and political participation? The term "gender gap" refers to differences between men and women in their political attitudes, beliefs, values, policy preferences, issue agendas, political party affiliations, and voting. If a gender gap exists, it may influence electoral outcomes and the public policies that elected and appointed officials create, amend, implement, enforce, and adjudicate. Journalists, politicians, and scholars continue to debate whether and to what extent a gender gap exists in political orientation and behavior, the reasons for its existence, and its consequences for politics and public policy.

In this chapter, "political orientation" refers to political beliefs, attitudes, and values and their expression through political action. Differences in political orientation can be viewed in two ways: as gender differences in political attitudes, beliefs, and values and as gender role differences. Gender roles, which are created by the culture and learned by individuals, are expectations about how individuals should behave; they have implications for attitudes, beliefs, and values that pertain to politics. In this chapter we will examine differences in political orientation both between women and men and among women who have different gender role perspectives.

As discussed in Chapter 2, gender consciousness as it relates to political behavior is "the recognition that one's relation to the political world is shaped in important ways by the physical fact of one's sex."[1] Elements of gender consciousness include identification with other members of the gender, positive feelings toward other members, perceptions of the gender group's advantage or disadvantage relative to other groups, and a sense of collective destiny.[2] Women who have gender consciousness may differ in their political orientation and political activity from women who do not.

When did the gender gap in political attitudes and policy preferences first emerge? Some say the 1950s. Certainly two social movements— women's liberation and the second wave of the feminist movement—and the birth of organizations to promote equality for women have influenced women's political attitudes and policy preferences. Those organizations advocate equal access to all aspects of higher education, equal employment opportunity (including equal access to jobs and equal pay and benefits for the same or similar work), and equal treatment of men and women in state and federal law.

Observers have offered several explanations for the gender gap in political attitudes and policy preferences. One is that women and men are socialized to different roles, with an accompanying difference in values. In this view, women are more compassionate, and men are more competitive and aggressive. A second is the increased economic opportunities available to women, made possible through expanded educational and employment opportunities brought about by changes in federal and state laws since the 1960s. A related explanation emphasizes social structural changes, such as the increased participation of women in the labor force. Many women work outside the home because they want to or because they desire higher standards of living for their families. Furthermore, the high divorce rate results in more women working to support their families. In addition, a greater proportion of never-married women in the population results in more women working to support themselves. Public policies may affect women differently depending on whether they work outside the home. For many women, these differences contribute to the development of gender consciousness.

EXPLAINING GENDER DIFFERENCES IN POLITICAL ORIENTATION

Some scholars have criticized research on men's and women's political orientation and political participation because the theories behind the research ignore gender roles. Why might gender roles result in different political orientations for men and women? One possible explanation is differences in children's political socialization—that is, as children males and females learn different orientations with regard to politics. Children are taught social roles by parents, teachers, religious leaders, social group leaders, and the mass media. Certain attitudes, beliefs, values, and behaviors are associated with those roles. Learning of social roles can be either direct or indirect (see Chapter 2). Before the 1960s, when the modern women's movement began to gain prominence, girls differed widely from boys in their political orientations. Girls were less interested in politics, had less political knowledge, and perceived those who wielded political authority—such as the president and the police—as benevolent figures.[3] Studies conducted in the 1960s and 1970s revealed that boys and girls continued to differ in some measures of political orientation. Cultural lags may exist because younger citizens are socialized by adults who were themselves socialized in a patriarchal society.[4]

More recent research suggests that gender differences in childhood learning about politics remain but have diminished over time. A 1985 study of students ages ten to seventeen found significant differences between males and females in approximately half the measures of politicization.[5] Another study surveyed high school seniors in 1972 and again in 1974 after their graduation. Females were found to have been more active in high school activities than males and more likely to believe in the value of the democratic process. However, when surveyed in 1976 and 1986, those same females were less likely to be active in politics than their male former classmates.[6] There are also generational differences, suggesting that women's support for feminist policies has changed over time. One comparison of mothers and daughters in the mid-1970s indicated that daughters were more supportive of a feminist agenda than were their mothers.[7]

Another explanation for gender differences in political orientation is the differential treatment of men and women in the law and in government rules and regulations. Although federal and state antidiscrimination and affirmative action laws enacted in the 1960s and 1970s outlawed sexual discrimination in employment, access to housing, and educational opportunities, subtle forms of discrimination still exist. Adult learning of the implications of gender roles may influence some women's political orientations. For example, women may develop an increased awareness of the differential treatment of women and men by employers and of restricted employment opportunities for women (including the "glass ceiling"—the label applied to employers' reluctance to promote women to senior management and professional jobs). The result of this learning process may be differences in political attitudes, beliefs, and values both between men and women and among women.[8]

Early gender role socialization may reinforce the perception of structured inequalities in educational attainment, occupation, and income. In the past women tended to have lower levels of educational attainment and fewer job opportunities. However, by 2001 a greater proportion of college-age women than of college-age men were enrolled in colleges and universities.[9] Differences in cultural orientation may also affect the political orientation of women.[10] For example, religious beliefs affect political orientation. The doctrines of many religions are based on patriarchal authority, although the degree to which women are proscribed from engaging in political activity varies. Women who are members of denominations that adopt a patriarchal view of women's roles would be expected to be less supportive of gender equality in government, business, and society. Evangelical women have been found to be less supportive of equal rights for women than nonevangelical women. Adherence to evangelical doctrine is also associated with opposition to abortion and decreased support for the women's movement as well as decreased support for government assistance to improve the socioeconomic status of women.[11] Although evangelical women as a group tend to be more conservative on women's issues, a substantial proportion of them support moderate positions.[12] Two-fifths believe that women should have an equal role with men, one-third support federal government efforts to improve the socioeconomic status of women, and one-sixth support abortion rights.[13]

GENDER DIFFERENCES
IN POLITICAL PREFERENCES

Women and men differ on several political attitudes and beliefs. They have different views on policy issues that relate to "compassion for others." Women are more supportive than men of the view that government should provide services and assistance to those who are less fortunate. Women and men also differ on the use of force: Women are more likely to support gun control, to oppose the use of force to resolve conflicts, and to support decreased government funding for military programs. Women and men differ in their views on affirmative action and sexual harassment and in their support for government efforts to deal with these problems. Men tend to be more politically knowledgeable than women, particularly with regard to the federal government and national politics. Women are more likely to identify with the Democratic Party and to support Democratic candidates; men tend to identify with the Republican Party. But few gender differences exist in attitudes and beliefs on abortion policy and the trustworthiness and effectiveness of the federal government.

Another controversial issue is that of allowing prayer in public schools. Approximately half of men and women surveyed every two years from 1986 to 1998 approved of public schools scheduling time when students could pray silently, while one-eighth indicated they were totally opposed to prayer in school. In 1998 women (28 percent) were more likely than men (20 percent) to support public schools scheduling time when children as a group could say a general prayer not tied to any particular religious faith. In that same year, a small minority of both men and women (8 percent) supported scheduling a time when all children would say a Christian prayer.[14]

Many organizations sponsor surveys that illuminate Americans' changing political orientations over time. By asking the exact same questions year after year, the annual survey conducted by the National Opinion Research Center of the University of Chicago and the biennial survey by the Center for Political Studies of the University of Michigan help us analyze patterns in men's and women's views on a number of policy issues as well as their political orientation.

Opinions on Policy Issues

Before we explore whether men and women differ in their policy preferences, we should ask, "Why does it matter?" Do policy preferences affect political behavior? In order for policy preferences to impact behavior, three requirements must be met. First, some fraction of the public must be divided on the issue. Second, the issue has to be important (salient) to at least some of those who hold different views on the issue. Third, candidates for office or the political parties must be perceived as taking different stands on that issue.[15] At least some issues in the political arena meet these conditions. The result is political activities that seek to influence the political decisions of the executive, legislative, and judicial branches. Issues that divide the public are also used as weapons in electoral campaigns, with each party or candidate trying to mobilize the adherents of the issue position and demobilize the opponents, or vice versa.[16] Through public opinion polls, campaign strategists identify which issues divide different groups and are important enough to be used in campaigns. Some of these issues appear in the following sections.

EXPANSION OF GOVERNMENT PROGRAMS AND SERVICES. One indicator of policy preferences is the level of support for increased government spending for a particular program or service. In a national study conducted in 1992, a representative sample of the U.S. electorate was asked questions designed to measure support for several types of public policies. The survey respondents were asked to place themselves on a seven-point continuum, ranging from strong support (for more spending and services) to strong opposition. One item was worded as follows:

> Some people think the government should provide fewer services, even in areas such as health and education, in order to reduce spending. Suppose these people are at one end at point one. Other people feel it is important for the government to provide services even if it means an increase in spending. Suppose these people are at the other end at point 7. And of course, some other people have opinions somewhere in between at points 2, 3, 4, 5, or 6. Where would you place yourself on this scale, or haven't you thought much about this?[17]

If those who support an increase (points 5, 6, and 7) are placed in one category and those who oppose an increase (points 1, 2, and 3) are placed in another, in 1992 men and women differed significantly on issues of government spending as measured by this scale. Forty-two percent of the women compared with 32 percent of the men supported provision of more services and increased spending in policy areas such as health and education; only 26 percent of the women, compared with 38 percent of the men, supported decreased spending. Questions on spending for specific programs revealed that women were more willing than men to increase spending for financial aid for college students, the homeless problem, aid to the poor, child care programs, crime prevention, environmental improvement, social security programs, and public schools. Women were less willing than men to decrease spending on welfare and urban assistance programs, but more willing to decrease foreign aid to the new countries that were part of the Soviet Union. Men were more supportive than women of increased federal spending for science and technology.[18]

Differences between men and women in support for government spending have persisted. In 2000 men were more supportive than women of increased spending for highways. Women were more supportive than men of increased spending for prevention of crime, provision of social security benefits, aid to poor people, support for public schools, and provision of child care. Men and women did not differ significantly in their levels of support for government spending for welfare, AIDS research, environmental programs, aid to racial and ethnic minorities, and aid to immigrants. Women are more supportive of increased spending on government services such as education and health, but less favorable of increased spending on defense programs. A majority of men, but not of women, believe that the government does not have an obligation to see to it that everyone has a job and a good standard of living. When asked if the government should provide fewer services, even in such areas as health and education, in order to reduce spending, or provide many more services, even if it means an increase in taxes, gender differences appeared in responses.[19] Thirty-one percent of men and 46 percent of women supported more government provision of services and higher levels of spending; only 22 percent of men and 13 percent of women supported decreases in government spending and services.[20]

A major issue in U.S. politics is how to provide access to adequate health care for all Americans. Support for a government insurance plan among both men and women has varied from the 1970s to today, with the proportion supporting a government plan ranging from 30 percent to 43 percent among men and 32 percent to 46 percent among women. In 2000, two-fifths of both men and women supported a government health insurance plan that would cover all medical and hospital expenses for everyone. In contrast, one third thought that individuals and private insurance plans should pay for medical and hospital expenses.[21]

Since the 1980s men have consistently been more supportive of increased spending on defense.[22] A plurality of both men and women surveyed in 1992 preferred to spend much less money on defense.[23] But when respondents were asked whether military strength should be maintained even if it would require continued high defense spending, women were significantly less likely than men to support such expenditures.[24] In 2000 women were also less supportive of an increase in military spending, with 39 percent of the women surveyed compared to 54 percent of the men agreeing that spending on the armed forces should increase.[25]

USE OF FORCE TO SOLVE PROBLEMS. Women and men differ in their readiness to approve of the use of force, as indicated by their responses to a variety of policy issues ranging from the death penalty to gun control to the use of U.S. troops to protect national security interests abroad. Women are consistently less supportive of the death penalty for persons convicted of crimes such as murder and more supportive of restrictions on possession of handguns.[26] Since the 1940s women have been less supportive of the use of force to maintain peace and stability abroad and more supportive of negotiated settlements.[27] Over the past fifty years, women have been slightly less likely than men to support U.S. involvement in efforts to solve world problems. In 2002, 24 percent of women and 18 percent of men agreed that "This country would be better off if we just stayed home and did not concern ourselves with problems in other parts of the world. " Seventy-five percent of women and 82 percent of men disagreed with that isolationist view of the world.[28]

ABORTION. A number of surveys have examined Americans' preferences on abortion policy. Because small differences in the wording of survey questions can result in significant variations in response patterns, an analysis of changes in opinion on abortion policy over time must be limited to comparing responses to the same question asked at different points in time. The General Social Survey has used the same question wording since 1972. The Center for Political Studies of the University of Michigan, in its biennial American National Election Study, used different wordings in 1972–1980 and in 1980–2000, so comparisons can also be made for each of those two periods.

Analysis of data from the General Social Survey indicates that since the mid-1980s there has consistently been strong public support for legalized abortion when the pregnancy would threaten the woman's health, when the fetus has a serious defect, or when pregnancy occurred as a consequence of rape or incest. The public has been much less supportive of abortion for other reasons, such as when the woman is married and does not want more children, when the family is poor and cannot afford to support any more children, or when the woman is not married and does not want to marry the father. (In one study, the first three circumstances are referred to as "traumatic abortion" and the last three as "elective abortion.") Since the 1970s public support has been much higher for traumatic abortions than for elective abortions.[29] Women are slightly less supportive of abortion than men, but the differences are very small. In 2000 only women and men ages thirty-six to forty-five differed in their support.[30]

Because the wording of the abortion attitude item in the American National Election Study survey changed between 1980 and 1984, it is difficult to examine changes in attitudes from 1972 to 2000. However, we can still make gender comparisons on this issue for each year and for a limited range of years. Tables 3-1 and 3-2 indicate the patterns of responses to the question of under what circumstances, if any, abortion should be permitted. The data lend themselves to three conclusions. First, men and women do not differ substantially in their views on this issue. Second, a plurality of Americans see abortion as a matter of personal choice. That was the policy preference of 42 percent of the men and 44 percent of the women surveyed in 2000. However, approximately 9–12 percent of men and 12–15 percent of women surveyed since 1980 have been opposed to abortion under any circumstances. Third, question wording does matter. In 1980, when both question wordings were presented to the same interviewees, more were found to support abortion rights when asked whether abortion was "a matter of personal choice" rather than whether it "should never be forbidden."

In 1992 a national survey asked respondents if they would favor or oppose a state law requiring parental consent before a minor (younger than eighteen) could have an abortion; 78 percent of men and 74 percent of women said they favored such a law. Forty-eight percent of men and 51 percent of women opposed the use of government funding to pay for abortions; 71 percent of men and 61 percent of women favored requiring a married woman to obtain her husband's permission before she could have an abortion.[31]

Attitudes toward abortion policy are related to political ideology and educational attainment. People who are more conservative tend to be less supportive of abortion. Educational attainment is the stronger predictor of

TABLE 3-1

Gender Differences in Opinion on Abortion, 1972–1980 (percent)

Opinion	1972		1976[a]		1980[a]	
	Men	Women	Men	Women	Men	Women
Abortion should never be permitted	10	12	11	11	9	10
Permit only when life and health of the woman are endangered	45	48	42	48	45	44
Permit if woman would have difficulty in caring for the child	18	17	18	16	21	16
Should never be forbidden	26	23	30	25	25	30

Sources: Calculated from data in University of Michigan, Center for Political Studies, "1952–1990 American National Election Studies Cumulative File."

[a] $p < .05$.

attitudes toward abortion, with those with less education being more strongly opposed to abortion.[32] One explanation is that higher levels of education increase tolerance for differing views.

AFFIRMATIVE ACTION. Prior to passage of the Civil Rights Act of 1964, discrimination based on sex, race, or other sociodemographic characteristics in hiring, promotion, distribution of benefits, and other conditions of employment was legal and widely practiced in the United States.[33] In 1972 Congress extended the act to include educational institutions in addition to employers. Also in 1972, Title IX of the Higher Education Act Amendments extended the prohibition against sexual discrimination in education to cover admissions and other aspects of educational programs.[34] At first, enforcement of these civil rights laws was passive, occurring only after a violation was reported to the enforcing agency. But during the late 1970s the enforcement focus began to shift to the initiation of affirmative action.[35] Affirmative action programs emphasize an open recruitment process, establishment of training and skills development programs for all employees, and promotion criteria that are based on employees' ability and performance. The necessity and fairness of affirmative action programs are controversial.[36]

TABLE 3–2
Gender Differences in Opinion on Abortion, 1980–2000 (percent)

Opinion	1980 M	1980 W	1984 M	1984 W	1988ᵃ M	1988ᵃ W	1992 M	1992 W	1994 M	1994 W	1996 M	1996 W	1998 M	1998 W	2000 M	2000 W
Abortion should never be permitted	11	12	12	14	10	14	9	12	10	14	12	14	9	15	10	14
Permit only in case of rape or incest or to save the life of the woman	32	33	28	32	33	33	28	28	33	29	32	27	30	31	32	30
Permit for other reasons, but only after need has been established	22	17	22	19	20	17	16	13	16	12	18	14	17	16	16	14
Matter of personal choice	36	37	38	35	36	35	47	47	41	45	40	46	43	38	42	44

Sources: Calculated from data in University of Michigan, Center for Political Studies, "1952–1990 American National Election Studies Cumulative File" and the 1992, 1994, 1996, and 2000 American National Election Studies.

Note: M=Men; W=Women.

ᵃ p < .05.

Efforts to determine whether the public supports affirmative action suggest that question wording influences the patterns of support or opposition. Some surveys indicate that most people oppose hiring less-qualified individuals on the basis of their race or sex, giving preference in admissions to educational programs to minorities, and setting aside a proportion of government contracts for minority-owned firms.[37] In 2002 a majority of Americans supported affirmative action programs "designed to help blacks, women, and other minorities get better jobs and education," and a majority also supported programs that "give special preferences to qualified blacks, women, and other minorities in hiring and education." However, upon examining the views of white men and white women on these issues, stark differences pop out. Two-thirds of white women favor programs that "help blacks, women, and other minorities get jobs and education," compared with 48 percent of men. When white men and women were asked if they have been helped or hurt by affirmative action programs, only 1 percent of white men and 3 percent of white women believe they have been helped, while 17 percent of white men and 9 percent of white women believe they have been hurt by affirmative action programs. Eighty-four percent of whites believe they have not been affected by these programs.[38] Support for affirmative action appears to vary with the context. Affirmative action for women appears to elicit more support than affirmative action that focuses on both minorities and women.

Opposition to giving special consideration to women in education and employment can be explained in part by the public's perception that things are better for women than they were twenty-five years ago. In a 1992 survey, only 6 percent of respondents said they thought women's opportunities were worse than they were twenty-five years ago; 79 percent said opportunities were somewhat better or much better.[39] However, in a 1994 survey, women were found to be slightly less likely than men to believe that women have an equal chance to succeed (59 percent of the women respondents compared with 64 percent of the men).[40] In another national survey carried out in 1995, women were asked if they had ever been discriminated against by not being offered a job; 19 percent of them responded yes, and 13 percent said they had been discriminated against in promotions.[41] Although women are much more supportive of affirmative action programs for women than are men in the same age group, among women the support is least strong among those ages thirty to forty-four; only 63 percent support affirmative action programs for women (see Table 3-3).[42]

TABLE 3-3

Gender Differences in Support for Affirmative Action Programs to Help Women Get Better Jobs and Education, by Age Group (percent)

Age group	Men		Women	
	Favor	Oppose	Favor	Oppose
18–29	55	22	73	9
30–44	48	35	63	24
45–64	59	31	75	9
65+	40	39	71	16

Sources: Los Angeles Times survey, March 15–19, 1995. Reported in *Public Perspective* 6, no. 4 (June/July 1995): 39.

Note: The question was: "Are you in favor of affirmative action programs designed to help women get better jobs and education, or are you opposed to them, or haven't you heard enough to say?"

However, support for affirmative action varies with the wording of the survey question, as is evident from a comparison of the pattern of responses to the question asking whether respondents support "affirmative action programs designed to help women get better jobs and education" (Table 3-3) to the response pattern when the question refers to giving preference in hiring or promotion "where there has been job discrimination against women in the past" (Tables 3-4 and 3-5). Support also varies by level of education. Respondents with some college or a college degree are generally less supportive, although within each educational grouping women are more supportive than men of giving preferences to women in hiring to overcome the results of past discrimination (see Table 3-5). Women are also more likely to believe that affirmative action programs are still necessary to protect women from discrimination, and that affirmative action programs designed to help women get better jobs and a better education do not go too far and are not adequate.[43]

Is there a white male backlash against affirmative action programs for women? A 1995 Louis Harris survey suggests that if such a backlash exists, it is not based on personal experiences in the workplace. When men were asked, "Do you feel that your employer has been doing too much, too little, or about the right amount to hire and promote women employees?" only 9 percent said "too much" and 11 percent said "too little"; 69 percent responded that their employer was "doing about the right amount."[44]

TABLE 3-4

Gender Differences in Support for Affirmative Action Programs in Hiring or Promotion of Women, by Age Group (percent)

Age group	Men		Women	
	Favor	Oppose	Favor	Oppose
18–29	37	63	54	42
30–44	37	58	52	39
45–64	35	61	51	41
65+	34	54	41	43

Sources: CBS/*New York Times* survey, April 1–4, 1995. Reported in *Public Perspective* 6, no. 4 (June/July 1995): 39.

Note: The question was: "Where there has been job discrimination against women in the past, preference in hiring or promotion should be given" to women?

Women in the military is another issue that concerns values relating to equality. Men and women differ in their attitudes on this issue. In a 1993 survey almost four-fifths of women and slightly more than half the men said they approved of allowing women to assume combat roles.[45]

SEXUAL HARASSMENT. Sexual harassment of women is not new; however, its importance as a political issue escalated with nomination of Clarence Thomas to the Supreme Court and the allegations presented at his confirmation hearings before the Senate Judiciary Committee in October 1991. Attorney Anita Hill, a former employee of the Equal Employment Opportunity Commission when it was chaired by Clarence Thomas, alleged that he had persistently harassed her. Feminists claimed that the all-male Judiciary Committee "did not get it," igniting a firestorm of controversy and focusing national attention on the problem of sexual harassment.[46] In 1992 the American National Election Study survey found that men and women differed significantly in their perception that sexual harassment was a serious workplace problem (38 percent of women compared with 25 percent of men). Women (41 percent) were more likely than men (31 percent) to report that they or someone they knew had experienced sexual harassment at work. A majority of the men and almost two-thirds of the women thought too little was being done to protect women from sexual harassment. When asked, "If a woman says she has been sexually harassed

TABLE 3-5

Gender Differences in Support for Affirmative Action Programs in Hiring or Promotion of Women, by Level of Education (percent)

	Men		Women	
Education	Favor	Oppose	Favor	Oppose
High school or less	42	53	55	35
Some college	23	74	48	41
College graduate	31	66	36	58

Source: CBS/*New York Times* survey, April 1–4, 1995. Reported in *Public Perspective* 6, no. 4 (June/July 1995): 39.

Note: The question was: "Where there has been job discrimination against women in the past, preference in hiring or promotion should be given" to women?

at work and the man denies it, would you be more inclined to believe the woman or the man?" Forty-four percent of the men and 62 percent of the women responded that they would be more likely to believe the woman. But 47 percent of the men and 34 percent of the women indicated it would depend on the circumstances related to the allegation.[47]

TRUSTWORTHINESS AND EFFECTIVENESS OF THE FEDERAL GOVERNMENT. To what extent do men and women differ in the trust they place in the federal government and in their sense of its political effectiveness? Table 3-6 shows responses to four survey questions, three of which were developed as measures of trust:

1. How much of the time do you think you can trust the government in Washington to do what is right—just about always, most of the time or only some of the time?
2. Would you say the government is pretty much run by a few big interests looking out for themselves or that it is run for the benefit of all the people?
3. Do you think the people in the government waste a lot of the money we pay in taxes, waste some of it, or don't waste very much of it?

Between 1964 and 1994, trust in the government in Washington plummeted among both men and women, especially as measured by responses to the first two questions. Trust in the government began to increase by 1995, with the trend continuing through 2002. Beginning in 1996 the proportion of both men and women believing that the government is run by a few big interests declined, with no substantial differences between the sexes. In 1996 the perception that the government wastes a lot of money also began to decline. Only infrequently have there been major gender differences in the responses to these questions.[48] In several years (1968, 1972, 1984, 1992, and 2002) women were much less likely than men to believe that the federal government wastes a lot of tax money. It could be that in general, women are more supportive of several types of domestic policy programs. Despite the few significant differences between men and women revealed by these responses, one pattern is clear: Trust in the federal government declined substantially from 1972 to 1994.

Another attitude indicative of what people think about government is their sense of political efficacy. This attitude has two components: (1) the feeling that people like oneself can be effective in politics (internal efficacy); and (2) the belief that the federal government is responsive to the views of people like oneself (external efficacy). Table 3-6 concerns one indicator of external political efficacy, a response to the statement that "I don't think public officials care much what people like me think." The proportion of survey respondents who say they believe that public officials don't care much "what people like me think" increased substantially between 1964 and 1994 and then declined. Only in 1996 and 2002 were there significant differences between men and women in their responses to this statement.

Measures of Political Orientation

Political orientations are shaped by a number of influences. In addition to parents, peer groups, and the mass media, education helps provide knowledge and develop critical thinking. Men and women differ in their political knowledge; men are more knowledgeable about both governmental processes and current events. Why might this be? Women are less likely to work outside the home or to have jobs that stimulate political interest and a feeling of political efficacy. In addition, in most families women have primary responsibility for child care, housework (cooking, cleaning, and doing the laundry), and elder care. They therefore have less time to acquire political information by reading newspapers and newsmagazines, watching television news, and engaging in political discussions.

TABLE 3-6
Gender Differences in Attitudes toward the Federal Government, 1964–2002 (percent)

Year	Trust the Government Most of the Time or Just about Always		Government Is Run by a Few Big Interests		Government Wastes a Lot of Money		Public Officials Do Not Care Much What People Think Like Me Think	
	Men	Women	Men	Women	Men	Women	Men	Women
1964	80	76	32	30	51	46	37	37
1968	62	63	49	39	66	56	42	45
1972	55	54	59	58	71	64	49	51
1976	36	34	74	73	77	76	52	55
1980	26	26	78	76	82	79	54	55
1984	43	46	60	57	72	62	42	43
1988	43	40	66	68	66	62	52	51
1992	28	30	79	78	72	65	53	52
1994	21	22	80	80	72	70	66	66
1996	34	31	72	72	62	58	64	58
1998	43	38	64	68	60	63	60	63
2000	44	44	65	65	61	59	56	54
2002	56	53	50	51	52	46	32	27

Source: Calculated from data in University of Michigan, Center for Political Studies, "1952–1992 American National Election Studies Cumulative File" and the 1994, 1996, 1998, 2000, and 2002 American National Election Studies.

As recently as 2002, women were less likely than men to have completed four or more years of college.[49] Thus we would expect women as a group to have less knowledge about the federal government's structure and processes. Women are as knowledgeable as men about local government and politics, however. When knowledge levels of women are compared to those of men with similar occupational status and levels of income and education, women are found to be less knowledgeable about national government and politics. One explanation is that many women were raised in families in which the gender role expectations for women did not include being interested in politics and being politically active.[50]

PARTY IDENTIFICATION. In the United States, a person's sense of identity with a political party affects how the person perceives qualities of candidates for elective office, evaluates the job performance of elected officials, and approves (or disapproves) of policies advocated by candidates, elected officials, and political party leaders. Gender differences in party identification began to develop in the early 1970s and have proved tenacious.[51] Since 1972 more women than men have reported an affiliation with the Democratic Party or have usually voted for candidates of the Democratic Party. The proportion of both men and women who declare themselves to be independent has varied since the 1950s. Gender differences in party identification can be explained in part by the movement of some men to the Republican Party beginning in the 1960s.[52]

During the 1990s gender differences in party identification were greatest among younger voters (ages eighteen to thirty-five); men were more likely to be Republicans and women more likely to be Democrats. Women college graduates in that age group were more likely to be Republicans than were women with less education, but they were less likely to be Republicans than college-educated men in the same age group.[53] By 2000 the greater divergence in party identification occurred among voters ages thirty-six to forty-five (see Figure 3-1).[54]

CANDIDATE PREFERENCE. One dimension of gender differences in political orientation is the evaluation of candidates for elective office. Gender differences in patterns of voting for president have been evident for decades. With the exception of 1976, when men and women were equally supportive of the Democratic Party's presidential candidate (Jimmy Carter), a gender gap in presidential election voting patterns has existed since 1964,

FIGURE 3-1
Party Identification by Gender, 1952–2002 (percent)

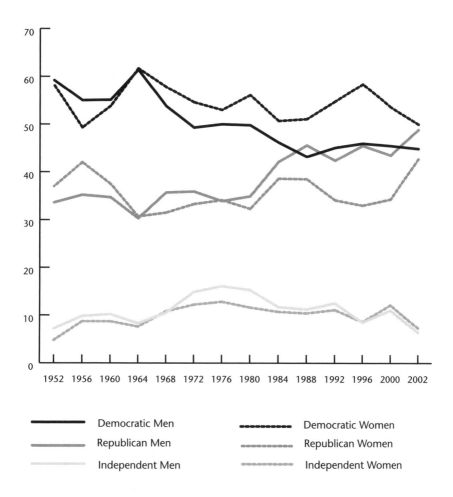

Source: University of Michigan, Center for Political Studies, "American National Election Studies Cumulative File 1948–2000," variable 303a; "American National Election Study, 2002," variable 023038x.

Note: Respondents were counted as identifying with a party regardless of whether they reported strong or weak ties to the party. Independents are those who did not identify with either party.

with women being more supportive of the Democratic Party's candidate.[55] However, support for the Democratic candidate varies with marital status; married women are less supportive than women who have never married or are separated or divorced. This "marriage gap" has also shown itself in varying support for Republican presidential candidates, with married women more likely to give support than nonmarried women. In 2000 the gender gap existed at every level of education, and it was largest among those with the lowest and highest levels of education. However, women in families with an income of $105,000 or more were more likely to vote for George W. Bush in 2000; those households represented less than 10 percent of women voting.[56]

Men and women also differ in their support for minor party and independent candidates. For example, in the 1990s men and women differed significantly in their evaluation of independent presidential candidate Ross Perot.[57] During the 1992 presidential election, women were significantly less likely than men to support Perot. In 1993 gender differences in evaluations of Perot continued. Women were significantly less likely to support him; the differences were particularly striking among younger voters. Republican men in all age groups were almost twice as likely as Republican women to support the former presidential candidate.[58] In the 2000 presidential election, Green Party candidate Ralph Nader received very little support, but a higher proportion of men than women reported voting for him.[59]

To what extent are women willing to support women candidates for elective office? Analyses of voting patterns suggest that, under certain conditions, women are more likely than men to vote for women candidates. In thirty-five statewide contests for the U.S. Senate or for a state governor from 1980 to 1990, the gender difference in voting patterns was 10 percent or greater. In five other contests, a plurality of women voted for the woman candidate and a plurality of men voted for the man. In all of these statewide races, Democratic women candidates usually attracted women's votes (sixteen out of nineteen contests); Republican women candidates attracted women's votes in only three of sixteen contests. The ability of Democratic women candidates to increase voter turnout and attract votes increased during the 1980s. During this period women were less supportive of Republican candidates than were men, regardless of the Republican candidate's gender. This gender gap was evident in presidential elections as well as in races for the U.S. Senate and in gubernatorial contests.[60]

SUGGESTIONS FOR FURTHER READING

In Print

Baxter, Janeen, and Emily W. Kane. 1995. "Dependence and Independence: A Cross National Analysis of Gender Inequality and Gender Attitudes." *Gender and Society* 9, no. 2 (April): 193–195.

Chaney, Carol Kennedy, R. Michael Alvarez, and Jonathan Nagler. 1998. "Explaining the Gender Gap in U.S. Presidential Elections." *Political Research Quarterly* 51, no. 2 (June): 311–339.

Clark, Cal, and Janet Clark. 1999. "The Gender Gap in 1996: More Meaning Than a 'Revenge of the Soccer Moms.' " In Lois Duke Whitaker, ed., *Women and Politics,* 3d ed. Upper Saddle River, N.J.: Prentice Hall, 68–84.

Gupte, Manjusha. 2002. "Gender, Feminist Consciousness, and the Environment: Exploring the 'Natural' Connection." In *Women and Politics* 24, no. 1: 47–62.

Kaufman, Karen M., and John R. Petrocik. 1999. "The Changing Politics of the Gender Gap." *American Journal of Political Science* 43, no. 3 (July): 864–887.

Manza, Jeff, and Clem Brooks. 1998. "The Gender Gap in U.S. Presidential Elections: When? Why? Implications?" *American Journal of Sociology* 103, no. 5 (March): 1235–1266.

Norrander, Barbara. 1999. "The Evolution of the Gender Gap." *Public Opinion Quarterly* 63, no. 4 (winter): 566–576.

Norris, Pippa. 2003. "The Gender Gap: Old Challenges, New Approaches." In Susan Carroll, ed., *Women and American Politics.* Oxford: Oxford University Press.

Sapiro, Virginia, and Pamela Johnston Conover. 2001. "Gender Equality in the Public Mind." In *Women and Politics* 22, no. 1: 1–36.

Sapiro, Virginia, and Pamela Johnston Conover. 1997. "The Variable Gender Basis of Electoral Politics: Gender and Context in the 1992 Election." *British Journal of Political Science* 27, no. 4 (October): 497–523.

Steeh, Charlotte, and Maria Krysan. 1996. "Trends: Affirmative Action and the Public, 1970–1995." *Public Opinion Quarterly* 60, no. 1 (spring): 128–158.

On the Web

The Center for Political Studies, University of Michigan. *www.isr.umich.edu/cps/.* This center conducts the American National Election Studies survey focusing on presidential and congressional elections and public opinion about candidates, political parties, attitudes toward government, and opinion on major issues.

The Gallup Organization. *www.gallup.com.* This organization conducts surveys each week on policy issues and politics in the United States.

The Pew Research Center for the People and the Press. *www.people-press.org.* The Pew Research Center collects survey data on public opinion relating to political campaigns and policy issues. The center also funds research studies on policy issues.

The Roper Center for Public Opinion Research, University of Connecticut. *www.ropercenter.uconn.edu/.* This center acts as a data archive for surveys conducted by survey data collecting organizations.

NOTES

1. Sue Tolleson-Rinehart, *Gender Consciousness and Politics* (New York: Routledge, 1992), 14.

2. See Patricia Gurin, "Women's Gender Consciousness," *Public Opinion Quarterly* 49 (1985): 143–163; Patricia Gurin, Arthur H. Miller, and Gerald Gurin, "Stratum Identification and Consciousness," *Social Psychology Quarterly* 43 (1980): 30–47; and Arthur H. Miller, Patricia Gurin, Gerald Gurin, and Oksana Malanchuk, "Group Consciousness and Political Participation," *American Journal of Political Science* 25 (1981): 494–511. Pamela Johnston Conover and Virginia Sapiro in "Gender, Feminist Consciousness, and War," *American Journal of Political Science* 37 (November 1993), argue that "the cognitive core of feminist consciousness is an awareness of and sensitivity to the unequal and gendered nature of society (empirical sexual equality), and a commitment to ending the inequalities (normative sexual equality)" (1084). Three aspects of feminist consciousness are measured: "a commitment to normative sexual equality, a feminist identity, and a sense of emotional bond with women" (1086).

3. See Herbert Hyman, *Political Socialization* (New York: Free Press, 1959); David Easton and Jack Dennis, *Children in the Political System* (New York: McGraw-Hill, 1969); Fred I. Greenstein, *Children and Politics* (New Haven: Yale University Press, 1965); and Robert E. Hess and Judith V. Torney, *The Development of Political Attitudes in Children* (Chicago: Aldine, 1967).

4. Diana Owen and Jack Dennis, "Gender Differences in the Politicization of American Children," *Women and Politics* 8, no. 2 (1988): 23–43.

5. Research conducted by Owen and Dennis in 1985 (Ibid., Table 1) indicated that in eight of fifteen politicization measures, no significant differences existed between young males and young females; seven of fifteen politicization measures showed no significant differences between older males and older females.

6. Sandra Bowman Damico, Alfonso J. Damico, and M. Margaret Conway, "Students Who Become Citizens: Schools and Democracy," paper prepared for the Youth 2000 Conference, University of Teesside, Middlesbrough, England, July 19–22, 1995.

7. Roberta S. Sigel and John V. Reynolds, "Generational Differences and the Women's Movement," *Political Science Quarterly* 94 (1979–1980): 635–648. The mothers and daughters were interviewed in 1975 and 1976.

8. Pamela Johnston Conover suggests that a feminist identity and consciousness, once developed, leads to a redefinition of the values instilled by earlier socialization and such factors as educational attainment, employment history, and family experiences. These changed values affect both the salience of political issues and issue preferences. See Conover, "Feminists and the Gender Gap," *Journal of Politics* 50 (November 1988): 984–1010.

9. In 2001, 6.9 million men and 9 million women were enrolled in degree-granting programs in colleges and universities. U.S. Department of Commerce, Bureau of the Census, *Statistical Abstract of the United States* (Washington, D.C.: 2003), Table 223, p. 151.

10. See C. Richard Hofstetter and William A. Schultze, "Some Observations about Participation and Attitudes among Single Parent Women: Inferences Concerning Political Translation," *Women and Politics* 9 (1989): 83–105; M. Kent Jennings, "Gender Roles and Inequalities in Political Participation," *Western Political Quarterly* 37 (1983): 364–385; Ronald B. Rapoport, "The Sex Gap in Political Persuading," *American Journal of Political Science* 25 (1981): 32–48; Virginia Sapiro, *The Political Integration of Women* (Urbana: University of Illinois Press, 1983); and Clyde Wilcox, "Black Women and Feminism," *Women and Politics* 10 (1980): 65–84.

11. It is adherence to evangelical doctrine, not the particular religious denomination, that has a significant impact. Only with regard to views on abortion does evangelical denomination attain statistical significance. See Clyde Wilcox and Elizabeth Adell Cook, "Evangelical Women and Feminism: Some Additional Evidence," *Women and Politics* 9 (1989): 27–49.

12. Clyde Wilcox, "Feminism and Anti-Feminism among White Evangelical Women," *Western Political Quarterly* 42 (1989): 147–160.

13. Wilcox and Cook, "Evangelical Women and Feminism," 35.

14. University of Michigan, "School Prayer (2) 1986–1998," *The NES Guide to Public Opinion and Electoral Behavior,* www.umich.edu/~nes/nesguide/toptable/tab4c_3b.htm, Feb. 26, 2004.

15. Angus Campbell, Philip E. Converse, Warren E. Miller, and Donald E. Stokes, *The American Voter* (New York: John Wiley and Sons, 1960), Chap. 8.

16. For discussions of the role of issues in politics, see David C. Leege, Kenneth D. Wald, Brian S. Krueger, and Paul D. Mueller, *The Politics of Cultural Differences* (Princeton: Princeton University Press, 2002); Steven E. Schier, *By Invitation Only* (Pittsburgh: University of Pittsburgh Press, 2000); John Kenneth White, *The Values Divide* (New York: Chatham House, 2003); Jeff Manza and Clem Brooks, *Social Issues and Political Change* (Oxford: Oxford University Press, 1999).

17. University of Michigan, Center for Political Studies, "1992 American National Election Study," variable 3701.

18. Ibid., variables 3726, 3728, 3729–3731, and 3813–3819 pertain to preferences on government spending for various policies.

19. University of Michigan, Center for Political Studies, "2000 American National Election Study," variables 675 to 687.

20. University of Michigan, "Government Services and Spending 1982–2000," in *The NES Guide to Public Opinion and Electoral Behavior,* www. umich.edu/~nes/nesguide/2ndtable/t4a_5_2.htm, Feb. 20, 2004.

21. University of Michigan, "Government Health Insurance 1970–2000," in *The NES Guide to Public Opinion and Electoral Behavior,* www.umich.edu/ ~nes/nesguide/toptable/tab4a_3.htm, Feb. 20, 2004.

22. University of Michigan, "Military Spending (2) 7-point scale 1980–2000," in *The NES Guide to Public Opinion and Electoral Behavior,* www.umich.edu/ ~nes/nesguide/2ndtable/t4d-3b_2.htm, Feb. 26, 2004.

23. University of Michigan, Center for Political Studies, "1992 American National Election Study," variables 3701, 3716, and 3707.

24. Ibid., variable 3603.

25. University of Michigan, "Military Spending."

26. "Women and the Use of Force," *Public Perspective* 5, no. 5 (July/August 1994): 96.

27. Ibid. See Robert Shapiro and Harpreet Mahajan, "Gender Differences in Policy Preferences: A Summary of Trends from the 1960s to the 1980s," *Public Opinion Quarterly* 50 (1986): 42–61. Shapiro and Mahajan found moderately large differences in preferences concerning the use of force. The salience of this issue for women appears to have increased over time. See also Tom Smith, "The Polls: Gender and Attitudes toward Violence," *Public Opinion Quarterly* 48 (1984): 384–396.

28. University of Michigan, "The United States Should Not Concern Itself with World Problems 1956–2000," in *The NES Guide to Public Opinion and Electoral Behavior,* www.umich.edu/~nes/nesguide/toptable/tab4d_1.htm, Feb. 26, 2004.

29. James A. Davis, Tom W. Smith, and Peter V. Marsden, *General Social Surveys, 1972–2002: Cumulative File,* 2nd ICPSR Version, September 2003. The terms "traumatic abortion" and "elective abortion" were first used in Elizabeth Adell Cook, Ted G. Jelen, and Clyde Wilcox, *Between Two Absolutes: Public Opinion and the Politics of Abortion* (Boulder, Colo.: Westview Press, 1992), 33–38, 48.

30. University of Michigan, Center for Political Studies, "2000 American National Election Study."

31. University of Michigan, Center for Political Studies, "1992 American National Election Study," variables 3732 and 3735–3740.

32. Cook, Jelen, and Wilcox, *Between Two Absolutes,* 48–49.

33. M. Margaret Conway, David W. Ahern, and Gertrude A. Steuernagel, *Women and Public Policy: A Revolution in Progress* (Washington, D.C.: CQ Press, 1995), 64–67.

34. Judith A. Baer, *Women in American Law* (New York: Holmes and Meier, 1991), 77–78.

35. Conway, Ahern, and Steuernagel, *Women and Public Policy,* 69; Dorothy McBride Stetson, *Women's Rights in the U.S.A.* (Pacific Grove, Calif.: Brooks/Cole, 1991), 168–173.

36. Baer, *Women in American Law,* Chap. 3; Susan Gleck Mezey, *In Pursuit of Equality: Women, Public Policy, and the Federal Courts* (New York: St. Martin's Press, 1992), chap. 4.

37. NBC/*Wall Street Journal* survey, March 4–7, 1995, reported in *Public Perspective* 6, no. 4 (June/July 1995): 33; CBS/*New York Times* survey, April 1–4, 1995, reported in ibid.; and Princeton Survey Research Associates survey, February 1–3, 1995, reported in ibid. The Pew Research Center for the People and the Press, "Conflicted Views of Affirmative Action," press release, May 14, 2003. The survey was conducted from April 30 to May 4, 2003.

38. The Pew Research Center for the People and the Press, "Conflicted Views of Affirmative Action," May 14, 2003, press release. The survey was conducted from April 30 to May 4, 2003.

39. Greenberg-Lake, The Analysis Group survey, May 26–June 8, 1992, reported in *Public Perspective* 6, no. 4 (June/July 1995): 34.

40. Roper Center survey, August 22–29, 1994, reported in ibid.

41. Gallup poll, March 17–19, 1995, reported in ibid.

42. *Los Angeles Times* survey, March 15–19, 1995, reported in ibid., 39.

43. CBS/*New York Times* survey, April 1–4, 1995, reported in ibid.; *Los Angeles Times* survey, March 15–19, 1995, reported in ibid., 41.

44. Humphrey Taylor, "The White Male Backlash, If It Exists, Is Not Based on Personal Experiences in the Workplace," Harris poll press release, Harris poll no. 44, July 17, 1995. Survey was conducted June 8–11, 1995.

45. *Los Angeles Times* survey, February 11–16, 1993, reported in *Public Perspective* 4, no. 5 (July/August 1993): 102.

46. According to the Sexual Harassment Guidelines issued by the Equal Employment Opportunity Commission, sexual harassment is a form of sexual discrimination. In the *Code of Federal Regulations,* 29 C.F.R. chap. 14, sec. 1604.11 (1996), sexual harassment is defined as follows:

> Unwelcome sexual advances, requests for sexual favors, and other verbal or physical conduct of a sexual nature constitute sexual harassment when (1) submission to such conduct is made either explicitly or implicitly a term or condition of an individual's employment, (2) submission to or rejection of such conduct by an individual is used as the basis for employment or academic decisions affecting such individual, or (3) such conduct has the purpose or effect of unreasonably interfering with an individual's work performance or creating an intimidating, hostile, or offensive working environment.

47. University of Michigan, Center for Political Studies, "1992 American National Election Study," variables 3741–3744.

48. University of Michigan, Center for Political Studies, "1948–2000 American National Election Studies Cumulative File," variables 0604 to 0606, 0609. University of Michigan, Center for Political Studies, "2002 American National Election Study," variables 025174, 025176, 025175, and 025172. In 1976 the first presidential election year after Richard Nixon resigned as president, a significantly smaller proportion of women (compared with earlier years) trusted the federal government most of the time or just about always. Nixon was facing the threat of impeachment charges brought by the House of Representatives and conviction by the Senate as a consequence of illegal activities by members of his campaign staff during the 1972 campaign and his participation in the cover-up of those activities. In 1964 and 1968, a significantly smaller proportion of women (compared with 1972 and later years) believed the government to be run by a few big interests.

49. U.S. Department of Commerce, Economics and Statistics Administration, Bureau of the Census, *Statistical Abstract of the United States, 2003* (Washington, D.C.: 2004), Table 228, p. 153.

50. Michael X. Delli Carpini and Scott Keeter, "The Gender Gap in Political Knowledge," *Public Perspective* 3, no. 5 (July/August 1992): 23–26.

51. Gallup Omnibus survey and CNN/*USA Today* survey, October 1991–May 1992, reported in *Public Perspective* 3, no. 5 (July/August 1992): 27–28.

52. Mary E. Bendyna and Celinda C. Lake, "Gender and Voting in the 1992 Presidential Election," in Elizabeth Adell Cook, Sue Thomas, and Clyde Wilcox, *The Year of the Woman* (Boulder, Colo.: Westview Press, 1994), 238–239; Jeff Manza and Clem Brooks, "The Gender Gap in U.S. Presidential Elections," *American Journal of Sociology* 103, no. 5 (March 1998): 1235–1266; Barbara Norrander, "The Evolution of the Gender Gap," *Public Opinion Quarterly* 63 no. 4 (winter 1999): 566–576; Karen M. Kaufman and John R. Petrocik, "The Changing Politics of American Men: Understanding the Sources of the Gender Gap," *American Journal of Political Science* 43, no. 3 (July 1999): 864–887.

53. *Public Perspective* 7, no. 5 (August/September 1996): 16.

54. University of Michigan, Center for Political Studies, "2000 American National Election Study."

55. University of Michigan, Center for Political Studies, "1948–2000 American National Election Studies Cumulative Data File."

56. University of Michigan, Center for Political Studies, "2000 American National Election Study."

57. Paul R. Abramson, John H. Aldrich, and David W. Rohde, *Change and Continuity in the 1992 Elections,* rev. ed. (Washington, D.C.: CQ Press, 1995), 136.

58. Gallup polls, March, April, and June 1993, reported in the American Enterprise, *Public Perspective* 4, no. 5 (July/August 1993): 98.

59. University of Michigan, Center for Political Studies, "American National Election Study, 2000," variable 1241. Among those who reported voting in the 2000 presidential election, 3.8 percent of men and 2 percent of women voted for Nader.

60. Tom Smith and Lance A. Selfa, "When Do Women Vote for Women?" *Public Perspective* 3, no. 6 (September/October 1992): 30–31.

CHAPTER 4

Differences among Women: Does Group Identification Explain Political Orientation?

Emily and Ashley are the same age, but their lives are very different. Emily graduated from high school and married after graduation. Only after both her children had entered elementary school did she take a job outside the home. She works as a cashier at a grocery store and does not expect to be promoted to a managerial position. Her job benefits are limited to an expensive health insurance plan. Ashley, on the other hand, graduated from college, married, and entered a management training program with a bank. She has received several promotions and is now a regional manager with the bank corporation. Her employer provides benefits that include a robust health insurance plan, retirement benefits, and paid maternity leave. She took maternity leave after each of her two children were born and then returned to work.

Ashley supports an equal role for men and women in business, government, and industry, whereas Emily believes that women should always be subordinate to men and should never have an equal role in decision making. Ashley believes the women's movement has made a major positive contribution to improving conditions for women; Emily opposes the women's movement. Ashley is an example of a feminist; Emily is an example of a nonfeminist.

PATTERNS OF GROUP CONSCIOUSNESS

A person's attitudes, beliefs, and behavior can be analyzed on the basis of the person's psychological identification with a particular group—otherwise known as their "group consciousness." To what extent do women identify with women as a group? Do women's political orientations and political activity vary with women's levels of group consciousness? The hypothesis examined here is that women who identify with other women have similar perceptions of the problems facing women and are more likely to engage in political and social actions that might alleviate those common problems. This shared identity is called gender consciousness. Women may have gender consciousness yet have different views of the problems that women encounter and the best solutions for those problems. For example, during the last decades of the twentieth century, the leaders of politically liberal women's groups such as the National Organization for Women and the Women's Equity Action League, which strive for equality of opportunity for women in society, business, and politics, have had very different views and policy preferences on many issues. Other women believe that women's place is in the home. Interest groups such as Conservative Women of America represent their point of view.

Components of Group Consciousness

The components of group consciousness include social group identification and the sharing of perceptions of problems and interests with other group members. Other components of group consciousness include being discontented with the group's power compared with that of other social groups, viewing perceived disparities as illegitimate, and having a collective orientation toward solving shared problems.[1] A label given to this kind of group consciousness among women is "feminist consciousness."

An indicator of the components of feminist consciousness is a survey item that has been included in the American National Election Studies since 1972:

> Recently there has been a lot of talk about women's rights. Some people feel that women should have an equal role with men in running business, industry, and government. Others feel that women's place is in the home. Where would you place yourself on this scale, or haven't you thought much about this?[2]

Support for an equal role for women is generally agreed to be a component of feminist consciousness. The opposite view of the appropriate role for women is that "women's place is in the home." This traditional view emphasizes the domestic roles of wife and mother in a patriarchal society, in which women are subordinate to men. It was predominant in American society until the second half of the twentieth century, when the perspective changed dramatically.

Table 4–1a shows the response patterns of women and men to the preceding question in surveys conducted in election years 1972 through 1996. Table 4–1b shows the responses to the same question asked in 2000, but fewer response categories were provided in 2000 than in earlier years. In 2000 a higher percentage of women (73 percent) than men (66 percent) placed themselves at the strongest level of support for an equal role for women. And if the two scores supporting an equal role for women (1 and 2) are added together, in 2000, 78 percent of men and 83 percent of women supported an equal role for women.

Studies using data from a panel study of individuals surveyed in 1973 and again in 1982 found a similar trend toward more support for an equal role for women.[3] Another study has found that for all individuals except those with the most limited cognitive ability, attitudes regarding equal roles are associated with patterns of political attitudes.[4]

Social Group Identification

The extent to which women feel close to other women is one measure of social group identification, a key component of group consciousness. The survey of the U.S. electorate conducted in national election years by researchers at the University of Michigan (the American National Election Study) includes an item that asks respondents to indicate which groups they feel close to; one of the groups listed is women. The survey then asks respondents which one group they feel closest to. Since 1972 the proportion of women who report feeling close to women as a group has ranged from 35 percent to 49 percent, and the proportion of women reporting they feel closest to women has ranged from 8.4 percent to 10.6 percent.[5] In 2000, when the American National Election Survey asked women in face-to-face interviews to identify those groups to which they felt close from a list of seventeen, 94 percent of women reported they felt close to women. In a phone survey, 73 percent of women said they felt close to women as a group.[6]

TABLE 4-1a
Continuum Ranking of Gender Differences in Support for Equal Role for Women, 1972–1996 (percent)

Ranking[a]	1972		1976		1980		1984		1988		1992		1996	
	M	W	M	W	M	W	M	W	M	W	M	W	M	W
1 (Equal role for women)	33	33	34	33	35	35	36	36	40	46	50	56	47	54
2	11	8	14	8	18	16	16	11	19	13	17	12	23	16
3	8	6	11	10	9	11	11	10	10	10	8	6	8	8
4	18	22	18	21	15	19	23	24	17	16	14	14	13	10
5	7	6	9	8	9	6	8	8	6	4	5	4	4	4
6	5	4	5	5	8	6	3	4	4	4	3	2	3	3
7 (Women's place is in the home)	18	21	9	14	6	7	4	7	5	7	3	4	2	4

Source: Calculated from data in the "1952–1992 American National Election Studies Cumulative File" and the 1996 American National Election Study.

[a] The question asked: "Recently there has been a lot of talk about women's rights. Some people feel that women should have an equal role with men in running business, industry, and government. Others feel that women's place is in the home. Where would you place yourself on this scale, or haven't you thought much about this?"

1 = strongest level of support for an equal role for women; 7 = strongest level of support for "women's place is in the home."

TABLE 4-1b

Continuum Ranking of Gender Differences in Support for Equal Role for Women, 2000 (percent)

Ranking[a]	Men	Women
1 Strongly support equal role for women	66	73
2 Support equal role	12	10
3 Other/Depends/Neutral	17	12
4 Place is in the home	2	2
5 Strongly believe women's place is in the home	3	3

Source: Calculated from the 2000 American National Election Study.

[a] The question asked: "Recently there has been a lot of talk about women's rights. Some people feel that women should have an equal role with men in running business, industry, and government. Others feel that women's place is in the home. Where would you place yourself on this scale, or haven't you thought much about this?"
1 = strongest level of support for an equal role for women; 5 = strongest level of support for "women's place is in the home."

Another way to measure the extent to which women identify with women as a group is to ask survey respondents to indicate their feelings toward a variety of groups by rating each group on a "feeling thermometer," whose readings range from 100 (the most positive) to zero (the most negative). A reading of 50 is neutral, readings of 51 and above are positive, and those of 49 and below are negative. From 1972 to 1984 women were asked to rate the "women's liberation movement," as the modern women's movement was called in the 1960s and 1970s; in 1988 and 1992 they were asked to rate "feminists";[7] in 1992, 1996, and 2000 they were asked to rate the "women's movement."[8] Group identification among women from 1972 to 2000 as measured by their ratings of three women's groups on the feeling thermometer is indicated by the absolute mean scores in the first row of Table 4-2. Of course, it would be preferable to have evaluations of the same group (either the women's liberation movement, feminists movement, or the women's movement) over time. However, beginning in 1988, either "feminists" or the "women's movement" (rather than the "women's liberation movement") was used in these surveys. In 1992, both the "women's movement" and "feminists" were used. Thus both sets of responses can be used to construct feminist consciousness scales, and the

TABLE 4-2
Feminist Consciousness among Women, 1972–2000

	Women's liberation movement				Feminists movement		Women's movement		
	1972	1976	1980	1984	1988	1992a	1992b	1996	2000
Absolute mean score (feeling thermometer)	45	53	62	63	62	61	61	62	64.1
Average equal role score	3.5	3.3	2.9	3.0	2.6	2.2	2.2	2.2	2.2
Distribution of feminist consciousness scores									
Not a feminist	63	53	43	48	37	29	29	15	35
Potential feminist	27	28	35	35	48	53	40	51	31
Feminist	10	19	22	17	14	18	30	34	33

Source: Calculated from data in University of Michigan, Center for Political Studies, "1952–1990 American National Election Studies Cumulative File" and the 1992, 1996, and 2000 American National Election Studies.

Note: Based on responses to equal roles question and feeling thermometer scores for the women's liberation movement (1972 to 1984), feminists movement (1988 and 1992a), and the women's movement (1992b, 1996, and 2000). A score of 1 on the equal roles item equals very strong support for an equal role for women, while the lowest score (7 in all years but 2000, 5 in 2000) equals strong support for the belief that women's place is in the home. Scores in 1992a and 1992b were pre- and postelection, respectively.

results obtained by using a different group in the surveys can then be compared.[9] These measures of feminist consciousness enable us to evaluate the extent of women's social group identification and the impact of feminist consciousness on patterns of political behavior and political attitudes.[10]

To evaluate the extent of women's feminist consciousness, we can analyze the patterns that appear when responses to questions on group closeness are combined with responses to questions pertaining to the equal role for women versus women's place is in the home. Sue Tolleson-Rinehart established three categories of women based on their responses to the group closeness questions: not close to other women, close, and closest.[11] The proportion reporting that they felt close to women ranged from 34 percent in 1972 to 62 percent in 1984. The proportion declined to 43 percent in 1988, and in 1992 it was 36 percent. By 2000, 72 percent of women reported feeling close to other women.[12] The proportion that reported feeling closest to women, of all the groups considered, ranged from 10.6 percent in 1976 to 6.7 percent in 1984.[13] In the years that this question was asked, the number of groups ranged from fifteen to nineteen.

The proportion of women who feel close to other women does not vary significantly with the employment status, marital status, family income, or education of those interviewed. However, in 2000 the proportion indicating they felt close to other women did vary by subjective social class, with women who considered themselves to be working class being less likely to report feeling close to other women. Women of color were less likely than were white women to report feeling close to other women.[14]

Although feeling close to other women is a component of gender consciousness, that alone does not indicate the existence of feminist consciousness. As was pointed out earlier, women may feel close to other women and yet have very different views about appropriate roles for women in society. Those who believe that women should not have an equal role have a "privatized" perspective on the preferred role for women.[15] Women may be gender conscious but not feminist. It is the interaction of different dimensions of attitudes that determines whether one is feminist.

Categories of Feminist Orientation

In examining the patterns of women's closeness to other women and their beliefs about an equal role for women, Tolleson-Rinehart established six categories of feminist orientation: individualist and privatized; identify with women and privatized; individualist and ambivalent; identify with women and ambivalent; individualist and egalitarian; and identify with women and egalitarian.[16] The proportion of women survey respondents who reported not feeling close to other women and who viewed women's appropriate role as being "in the home" decreased from 22.8 percent in 1972 to 7.9 percent in 1988; the proportion who reported not feeling close to other women but who were supportive of an equal role for women increased from 31.1 percent in 1972 to 43.4 percent in 1988. As might be expected, among those who reported feeling close to other women and those who said they felt closest to women, the proportion believing that women's place is in the home declined, whereas the proportion supporting an equal role for women increased.[17] Tolleson-Rinehart argues that changes in women's gender consciousness (traditional, ambivalent, or feminist) influence women's political beliefs and attitudes, political activity, and support for policy measures. Her research supports that argument.[18]

Women's gender consciousness derives from their beliefs about appropriate roles for women. Those who have feminist consciousness are aware of women's traditionally subordinate roles in society and the discrimination against women in a variety of social roles. Resentment of that pattern of discrimination may give rise to a collective orientation. However, other outcomes are also possible. Some women admit that women in general have suffered as a result of systematic discrimination but consider themselves to be exceptions. Roberta Sigel calls this the "not me" coping strategy. Another coping strategy is to "work harder" and excel on one's own. Women who adopt these approaches do not develop a collective orientation.[19]

An alternative method for evaluating feminist consciousness is to use the feeling thermometer ratings of the labels for the modern women's movement in combination with the scores indicating level of support for an equal role for women. Proponents of this method, which was developed by Elizabeth Adell Cook, point out that people differ in how positively they rate all groups, whereas an increase in the proportion of women who report they feel close to other women has been evident since the early 1970s. In addition, the closeness measure does not correlate highly with other components of group consciousness (discontent, system blame, and collective orientation) or with the feeling thermometer measure for the women's liberation movement.[20]

We can explore the extent to which women differ in their political participation by using this alternative measure of feminist consciousness. The feeling thermometer score must be adjusted for individuals' tendencies to vary in the ratings they give to groups. To do so, we create a mean feeling thermometer score by adding together the ratings given to nine groups (big business, labor unions, whites, blacks, liberals, conservatives, the military, poor people, and civil rights leaders) in the years before 1992. (Since 1988 the civil rights leaders measure has not been in the survey.) We then divide that score by the number of groups rated. Thus the equation to calculate this component of the feminist consciousness score looks like this:

Mean feeling thermometer score =sum of ratings of each of the groups divided by the number of groups (eight from 1992 to 2000; nine in prior years)

Some individuals tend to give high (or low) ratings to all groups. Therefore, the feeling thermometer rating given by each individual to the women's group label (the women's liberation movement, feminists, or the women's movement) must be adjusted in accordance with that individual's rating patterns. We use the following formula:

$$\frac{\text{Individual's rating of the women's group label} - \text{Individual's mean rating of all groups}}{\text{Individual's mean rating of all groups}}$$

The result is an index score. If an individual's rating of the women's group label is equal to the individual's mean rating of all eight (or nine) groups, her relative rating of the women's group rating is neutral or zero. If her relative rating of the women's group label is higher, the result will be a positive score. If it is lower, the result will be a negative score. Using the same criteria used by Cook, we will define an individual's rating of the women's movement as negative if it is 10 percent or more below the individual's mean rating of all groups.[21]

This index score, or relative feeling thermometer rating, is combined with the individual's score on the equal role question to create a feminist consciousness measure. The equal role question requires survey respondents to place themselves on a seven-point scale, with a score of 1 indicating support for an equal role for women and 7 indicating agreement with the statement that "women's place is in the home." Women who place themselves at 4 (neutral) or at 5, 6, or 7 (believe that women's place is in the home) are classified as lacking feminist consciousness. In 2000 the scale ranged from 1 to 5 with 3 being the neutral ranking. Women who place themselves at 1 or 2 (favor an equal role for women) and whose rating of the women's group label is at least 10 percent above their mean rating of other groups are classified as feminists. Those who favor an equal role for women but whose rating of the women's group is less than 10 percent of their mean rating of other groups are classified as potential feminists. Women who are not classified as feminists or potential feminists are labeled as nonfeminists.

Changing Patterns of Feminist Consciousness

The pattern of feminist consciousness has changed over time. The distribution of feminist consciousness scores and women's scores on the feeling thermometer in presidential election years 1972 to 2000 are shown in Table 4-2. Use of the measure based on ratings of the women's liberation movement, from 1972 to 1984, reveals a sharp drop in the proportion of women who lack feminist consciousness: from 63 percent in 1972 to 48 percent in 1984. There was a corresponding increase in the proportion of women with a potential for feminist consciousness: from 27 percent in 1972 to 35 percent in 1984.[22] If we use the measure based on ratings of feminists from 1988 to 1992, we note a similar trend: the proportion of nonfeminists declined and the proportions of potential feminists and feminists increased. The proportion of women who can be classified as feminists using the women's movement indicator increased from 1992 to 1996, then remained nearly constant in 2000. Using the measure of feminist consciousness based in part on evaluations of the women's movement in 2000, 35 percent of the women surveyed were nonfeminists, 31 percent were potential feminists, and 33 percent were feminists. Among the explanations for the relative stability in the proportions of those classified as feminists over time are that the women's movement may have received less attention in the mass media in more recent years and the gains in opportunities for women in education, business, government, and society are perhaps taken for granted.

What sociodemographic characteristics distinguish feminists from potential feminists and these two groups from nonfeminists? Support for feminism varies with women's age. Women ages eighteen to thirty-seven were strongest in their support for feminism; one-third can be categorized as feminists.[23] Feminist support also varies with education. Those with more education are more likely to be feminists.[24] Feminist support among married women in the sample varies with the spouse's education; those whose husbands are high school graduates or attended college are more likely to be feminists compared with those whose husbands did not graduate from high school.[25] Support for feminism also varies with employment status. In 2000, 25 percent of the employed women, 21 percent of the unemployed women seeking work, 45 percent of women working in temporary jobs, and 31 percent of the full-time students could be classified as feminists. In comparison, only 19 percent of homemakers are classified as feminists.

Women employed in executive, administrative, managerial, and technical jobs are more likely to be classified as feminists.[26]

RELATIONSHIP BETWEEN FEMINIST ORIENTATION AND POLITICAL ATTITUDES AND POLICY PREFERENCES

Do women's political attitudes and political participation vary with their support for feminism? If so, is the pattern consistent across attitudinal categories, or do attitudes vary with the issue? [27]

Support for Federal Government Programs

To examine the extent to which political attitudes and policy preferences vary with women's feminist consciousness, we can use some of the policy preference questions that were included in the 2000 American National Election Study. Citizens of voting age were asked if they would prefer to have the federal government spend more money, less money, or the same amount of money on a particular program. Women vary (categorized as feminists, potential feminists, and nonfeminists) in their support for federal spending for child care, environmental programs, aid to public schools, and using the projected budget surplus to support Social Security and Medicare (the surplus projected in 2000 has since turned into a large deficit).[28] Feminists were more supportive than potential feminists or nonfeminists of increased federal funding for all but the use of the surplus to support the Social Security and Medicare programs. Feminists did not differ significantly from other categories in support for funding for dealing with crime, aid to the poor, foreign aid, building and repairing highways, and spending on food stamps to the poor.[29] On the question of increasing federal spending, if necessary, to maintain the United States as the world's preeminent military power, nonfeminists were more supportive than potential feminists, and potential feminists were more supportive than feminists.[30] With regard to increased federal spending on health care and education in general, nonfeminists were the least supportive, and feminists were the most supportive.[31] When the question asked about government-sponsored health insurance, nonfeminists were the least supportive and feminists were the most supportive.[32]

A major problem for employed women with young children is finding good child care that is affordable. Women differ in their support for increased federal spending for child care assistance to low- and middle-income parents. However, a majority of each group in this study believed that the government should provide more funding: 52 percent of the nonfeminists, 66 percent of the potential feminists, and 73 percent of the feminists.[33]

Abortion Policy

The most significant differences of opinion on policy among women concern abortion. Tables 4-3 and 4-4 show differences in abortion attitudes among women categorized on the basis of a measure of feminist group consciousness. In 2000, 62 percent of the feminists, 44 percent of the potential feminists, and 33 percent of the nonfeminists agreed that "by law, a woman should always be able to have an abortion as a matter of personal choice."[34] The proportion of nonfeminists who believed abortion should be a matter of personal choice increased to 33 percent in 2000 from 24 percent in 1980. However, as Table 4.4 illustrates, the opinions of potential feminists and feminists on abortion have remained remarkably stable. Among potential feminists, the proportion supporting abortion as a matter of personal choice increased from 42 percent to 44 percent over that twenty-year period from 1980 to 2000, while feminists saw their support decrease slightly from 66 percent to 62 percent.

In 2000 a majority of all three groups believed that a minor should not be able to have an abortion without parental consent. Eighty-five percent of nonfeminists, 68 percent of potential feminists, and 60 percent of feminists supported a policy requiring parental approval before a teenager younger than eighteen can have an abortion.[35] A majority of each group also supported a law banning "partial birth abortions."[36]

How important an issue is abortion? When asked this in 2000, 68 percent of feminists, 63 percent of potential feminists, and 68 percent of nonfeminists indicated it was very important.[37]

TABLE 4-3
Women's Opinions on Abortion by Feminist Category, 1972–1980 (percent)

Opinion	1972			1976			1980		
	Non-feminist	Potential feminist	Feminist	Non-feminist	Potential feminist	Feminist	Non-feminist	Potential feminist	Feminist
Should never be permitted	14	5	7	13	8	4	16	6	1
Permit only if the life and health of the woman is in danger	55	43	28	59	44	22	56	44	22
Permit if woman would have difficulty in caring for the child	15	23	19	12	19	20	12	20	16
Should never be forbidden	16	29	46	16	29	54	16	30	60

Source: Calculated from data in University of Michigan, Center for Political Studies, "1952–1990 American National Election Studies Cumulative File."

TABLE 4-4
Women's Opinions on Abortion by Feminist Category, 1980–2000 (percent)

Opinion	1980			1984			1988			1992			1996			2000		
	N	P	F	N	P	F	N	P	F	N	P	F	N	P	F	N	P	F
Should never be permitted	20	8	2	20	9	5	22	9	5	21	10	5	29	12	7	22	12	6
Permit only in case of rape, incest, or when the woman's life is in danger	43	32	15	40	25	18	42	31	17	40	28	17	42	30	14	32	29	20
Permit for other reasons, but only after need has been established	14	18	17	18	24	16	16	21	14	14	17	10	13	14	12	13	15	13
Matter of personal choice	24	42	66	22	43	60	19	39	64	25	46	68	16	44	67	33	44	62

Source: Calculated from data in University of Michigan, Center for Political Studies, "1952–1990 American National Election Studies Cumulative File" and the 1992, 1996, and 2000 American National Election Studies.

Note: N=Nonfeminist; P=Potential feminist; F=Feminist.

Sexual Harassment

The 1992 study revealed that one-third of both the nonfeminists and potential feminists and almost half of the feminists believe that sexual harassment of women in the workplace is a very serious problem.[38] Moreover, a quarter of the nonfeminists, two-fifths of the potential feminists, and three-fifths of the feminists reported that they or someone they know had been sexually harassed in the workplace.[39] A majority of both nonfeminists and potential feminists and three-fourths of the feminists said they thought too little is being done to protect women from sexual harassment in the workplace.[40] When asked, "if a woman says she has been sexually harassed at work and the man denies it, would you be more likely to believe the woman or the man?" 53 percent of the nonfeminists, 60 percent of the potential feminists, and 68 percent of the feminists reported they would be more likely to believe the woman. An extremely small proportion reported they would be inclined to believe the man.[41]

ASSESSING THE POLITICAL IMPLICATIONS OF DIFFERENCES IN POLICY PREFERENCES

Although men and women differ widely in their policy preferences on several issues, women also differ among themselves. Many of these differences have persisted over time. If these differences in policy preferences are communicated to public officials, the impact on policy making, implementation, and enforcement can be significant.

Equally as important as policy direction, but infrequently or inadequately measured in many surveys, is the salience of policies—the relative importance of the policy to the respondent. For example, the availability, quality, and cost of child care facilities is of greater salience to employed parents of two small children than to an employed person with no children.

The intensity of policy preferences is no more frequently measured. Some individuals may consider a policy important but do not have intense feelings about it; others for whom that policy is also important may feel very strongly about it. The latter individuals are more likely to engage in political activity to persuade other citizens and policy makers. Unfortunately, the unavailability of survey data with which to measure policy saliency and the intensity of policy preferences on most of the policy issues examined here hinders any prediction of the implications for political action.

We have seen that women with differing degrees of feminist group consciousness also differ in their policy preferences. Another point of diversion of opinion is how best to solve the problems that are perceived as affecting women's status. In 1992 women were asked how women as a group might best improve their status. Two alternatives were presented: (1) each woman should attempt to become better trained and more qualified; and (2) women should work together. Sixty-three percent said that women need to work together.[42]

Some of the gender differences in political orientation and the differences among women based on their feminist orientation are not as large as those revealed when the data are analyzed on the basis of other characteristics, such as marital status, income, religion, and place of residence. An argument can be made that differences in vote choice are greater when the focus is on marital status, income grouping, or type of occupation than when gender alone is studied.[43]

Chapter 5 seeks answers to several questions. Do men and women engage in different types of political activities? Do they differ in the extent of their political participation? Are feminists more likely to be politically active than nonfeminists? Do all women participate in the same kinds of political activities, or do their activities differ according to feminist type? What is the likelihood that women can work together to find solutions to some of the policy problems discussed in this chapter?

SUGGESTIONS FOR FURTHER READING

In Print

Bennett, Linda L. M., and Stephen E. Bennett. 1999. "Changing Views about Gender Equality in Politics: Gradual Change and Lingering Doubts." In Lois Duke Whitaker, ed. *Women in Politics.* 3d ed. (Upper Saddle River, N.J.: Prentice Hall), 33–44.

Collins, Patricia Hill. 1991. *Black Feminist Thought: Knowledge, Consciousness, and the Politics of Empowerment.* (New York: Routledge).

Cook, Elizabeth Adell. 1999. "The Generations of Feminism." In Lois Duke Whitaker, ed. *Women in Politics.* 3d ed. (Upper Saddle River, N.J.: Prentice Hall), 45–55.

Held, Virginia. 1993. *Feminist Morality: Transforming Culture, Society, and Politics* (Chicago: University of Chicago Press).

Kelly, Rita Mae, and Jayne Burgess. 1989. "Gender and the Meaning of Power and Politics." *Women and Politics* 9, no. 1: 47–82.

Tolleson-Rinehart, Sue. 1992. *Gender Consciousness and Politics.* (New York: Routledge).

On the Web

All Women Count. *www.allwomencount.net.* All Women Count is the web page of the International Wages for Housework Campaign and of Win Wages (Women's International Network for Wages for Caring Work). The organizations' goal is to make visible the work of women and girls everywhere.

American Association of University Women. *www.aauw.org.* The American Association of University Women, which has more than 100,000 members, 1,300 branches, and 550 college and university partners nationwide, is one of the nation's leading voices promoting education and equity for women and girls. The AAUW Educational Foundation provides fund for research into issues of significance to women and girls in education.

Feminist Majority Foundation. *www.feminist.org.* The Feminist Majority Foundation (FMF) seeks to advance women's equality, nonviolence, economic development, and the empowerment of women and girls. All programs of the FMF endeavor to include a global perspective and activities to promote leadership development, especially among young women.

Institute for Women's Policy Research. *www.iwpr.org.* The Institute for Women's Policy Research is a public policy research organization dedicated to informing and stimulating the debate on public policy issues of critical importance to women and their families. Concentrating on such social and economic issues as poverty and welfare, employment and earnings, work and family issues, health and safety, and women's civic and political participation, the institute works with policy makers, scholars, and public interest groups to build a network of individuals and organizations that conduct and use women-oriented policy research.

National Organization for Women. *www.now.org.* The National Organization for Women (NOW) is the largest organization of feminist activists in the United States with a half million members and 550 chapters. NOW's goal has been to bring about equality for all women by eliminating discrimination and harassment in the workplace, schools, the justice system, and all other sectors of society.

NOTES

1. See Elizabeth Adell Cook, "Measuring Feminist Consciousness," *Women and Politics* 9, no. 3 (1989): 71–88; Ethel Klein, *Gender Politics* (Cambridge, Mass.: Harvard University Press, 1984); Patricia Gurin, "Women's Gender Consciousness," *Public Opinion Quarterly* 49 (1985); Patricia Gurin, Arthur H. Miller, and Gerald Gurin, "Stratum Identification and Consciousness," *Social Psychology Quarterly* 43 (1980); Arthur H. Miller and others, "Group Consciousness and Political Participation," *American Journal of Political Science* 25 (1981); and Sue Tolleson-Rinehart, *Gender Consciousness and Politics* (New York: Routledge, 1992).

2. University of Michigan, Center for Political Studies, "1948–2000 American National Election Studies Cumulative File Codebook," variable vcf0834.

3. Gregory B. Markus, "Stability and Change in Political Attitudes: Observed, Recalled, and 'Explained,' " *Political Behavior* 8 (1986): 21–44. The data were drawn from a three-wave panel study of high school seniors and their parents who were interviewed in 1965, 1973, and 1982.

4. Claire K. Fulenwider, *Feminism in American Politics: A Study of Ideological Influence* (New York: Praeger, 1980).

5. Tolleson-Rinehart, *Gender Consciousness and Politics,* Table 3.2, 55; University of Michigan, Center for Political Studies, "1992 American National Election Study," variable 6213. In 1992, 44 percent of the women responding to the survey said they felt close to women and 14 percent said they felt close to feminists (variable 6207). However, 10 percent of the women said that, of the fifteen groups listed, they felt closest to women; only 1 percent said they felt closest to feminists (variable 6218). In response to another survey item, 27 percent said they thought of themselves as feminists (variable 6002), and of those women 44 percent said they considered themselves to be strong feminists (variable 6003).

6. University of Michigan, Center for Political Studies, "2000 American National Election Survey," variables 001566 and 001567.

7. Calculated from data in University of Michigan, Center for Political Studies, "1952–1990 American National Election Studies Cumulative File," variable 225; "1992 American National Election Study," variable 5317 (feminists).

8. University of Michigan, Center for Political Studies, "1992 American National Election Study," variable 5324; "1996 American National Election Study," variable 961306; and "2000 American National Election Study," variable 001318.

9. There are problems with these measures of feminist consciousness, regardless of whether they are based on the feeling of closeness to women or on the feeling thermometer evaluations of the women's liberation movement, feminists, or the women's movement. But such measures are the best available for use over several decades and for national samples. The term "women's liberation movement" is rarely used today. In 1988 the American National Election Study substituted for it the term "feminists." That term has a negative connotation for many women, even

though they respond positively to the issue concerns and policy agenda of the women's liberation movement. In 1992 the feeling thermometers measured affective orientations toward both "feminists" and the "women's movement." For a discussion of the problem and scales designed to measure the four elements of women's gender consciousness, see Kenneth W. Mease, "Group Consciousness, Social Movements, and Political Participation" (Ph.D. diss., University of Florida, 1995).

10. Tolleson-Rinehart asserts that it is incorrect to divide those who are gender conscious into two groups based on their positive or negative evaluations of the "women's liberation movement." She argues that "consciousness is fundamentally cognitive, not affective, and it is a process, not an endorsement. Those who *are* gender conscious might certainly form attitudes toward the Women's Movement. . . , but such attitudes should be seen as a possible result of consciousness, and not of gender consciousness itself. To put it another way, a gender conscious woman would see the Women's Movement as a *means* (or block) to the overarching policy ends her consciousness constrains her to take—but she might not" (*Gender Consciousness and Politics,* 45).

11. The women were given the following instructions: "Here is a list of groups. Please read over the list of groups and tell me the letter for those groups you feel particularly close to—people who are most like you in their ideas and interests and feelings about things." Then each respondent was asked: "Of the groups you just mentioned, which one do you feel closest to?" See University of Michigan, Center for Political Studies, "1992 American National Election Studies Codebook," variables 6201 and 6218.

12. Tolleson-Rinehart, *Gender Consciousness and Politics,* Table 3.2, 55. Her analysis, covering the years 1972–1988, was based on data from University of Michigan, Center for Political Studies, 1972, 1976, 1980, 1984, and 1988 American National Election Studies. The 2000 data are from the American National Election Study, 2000.

13. Tolleson-Rinehart, *Gender Consciousness and Politics,* Table 3.2, 55. Her analysis, covering the years 1972–1988, was based on data from the 1972, 1976, 1980, 1984, and 1988 American National Election Studies and the 1992 American National Election Study. The "closest" response was not included in the 2000 American National Election Study.

14. University of Michigan, Center for Political Studies, "2000 American National Election Study," variables 000909, 000913, 000918, 001005, and 001006a.

15. The term "privatized" was used in this context by Virginia Sapiro in *Political Integration of Women* (Urbana: University of Illinois Press, 1983), 30–31; see Tolleson-Rinehart, *Gender Consciousness and Politics,* chap. 5.

16. In effect, this is a two dimensional conceptual scheme. The first dimension is whether women are individualistic (not close to other women) or identified (close to other women). The second dimension is whether women focus on the

private sphere (believe that a woman's place is in the home), the public sphere (women should have an equal role in business, industry, and government), or are ambivalent about the role women should take. Tolleson-Rinehart uses the resulting six categories in examining the relationship between gender consciousness and political variables such as patterns of vote choice in presidential elections, policy concerns, and policy preferences. See Tolleson-Rinehart, *Gender Consciousness and Politics,* chap. 6.

17. Tolleson-Rinehart, *Gender Consciousness and Politics,* Table 4.1, 79.

18. Ibid., 80–81; see also chaps. 4, 5, and 6.

19. Roberta S. Sigel, "Female Perspectives of Gender Relations" (paper presented at the annual meeting of the Midwest Political Science Association, Chicago, April 1988), cited in ibid., 46–47.

20. Cook, in "Measuring Feminist Consciousness," 77–80, makes a strong argument for using the feeling thermometer measure rather than the closeness measure to evaluate feminist consciousness, claiming that the feeling thermometer measure is adequate and accurate in meaning. She reports that the equal role measure also correlates more strongly with the feeling thermometer measure than with the closeness measure. The data used were collected from a national sample taken in 1976. In a factor analysis of the feeling thermometer scores, those for the women's liberation movement, measures of discontent, system blaming or withdrawal of legitimacy, collective orientation, and the equal role for women item all loaded on the same factor in a principal components analysis. The feeling thermometer measure was more strongly linked to other measures of feminist consciousness than was the closeness measure.

21. Cook, "Measuring Feminist Consciousness," 77.

22. It should be noted that because different labels are used in the analysis, trends are best measured in a time frame in which the measure is based on the same label.

23. Age categories (in years) used in the analysis were: eighteen to thirty-seven, thirty-eight to fifty-two, fifty-three to seventy-five, and older than seventy-five.

24. University of Michigan, Center for Political Studies, "2000 American National Election Study," variable 000917.

25. Ibid., variable 000917.

26. Ibid., variable 000969.

27. Prior research using other measures of feminist orientation suggests that political attitudes vary with gender role orientation. Elizabeth Adell Cook, Ted G. Jelen, and Clyde Wilcox, using data from the General Social Survey, developed two measures of gender role orientation: public aspects of gender roles, based on questions about the appropriate role orientations for women in government and business; and private aspects of gender roles, based on individuals' views of the appropriate role orientations for women, such as wife and mother. Attitudes concerning a number of policy issues varied with the feminism measures based on

private and public gender role orientations. Attitudes toward abortion also varied with attitudes regarding the desirability of having children, female employment, and sexual morality. See Elizabeth Adell Cook, Ted G. Jelen, and Clyde Wilcox, *Between Two Absolutes: Public Opinion and the Politics of Abortion* (Boulder, Colo.: Westview Press, 1992), Tables 3.3–3.6, 79–84.

28. University of Michigan, Center for Political Studies, "2000 American National Election Study," variables 000685, 000682, 000683, and 000693.

29. Ibid., variables 000684, 000680, 000678, 000675, and 000679.

30. Ibid., variable 000587.

31. Ibid., variable 000550.

32. Ibid., variable 000614.

33. Ibid., variable 000685.

34. Ibid., variable 000695.

35. Ibid., variable 000702.

36. Ibid., variable 000705.

37. Ibid., variable 000695.

38. University of Michigan, Center for Political Studies, "1992 American National Election Study," variable 3741.

39. Ibid., variable 3742.

40. Ibid., variable 3743.

41. Ibid., variable 3744.

42. Ibid., variable 6004.

43. Richard L. Berke, "Voting Differences by Sex Are Overplayed, Study Says," *New York Times,* August 24, 1995, B15. The study's research was sponsored by the National Women's Political Caucus.

CHAPTER 5

Women's Political Participation

Political participation is the cornerstone of democracy. As Robert Dahl states in *Democracy and Its Critics:*

> Throughout the process of making binding decisions, citizens ought to have an adequate opportunity, and an equal opportunity, for expressing their preferences as to the final outcome. They must have adequate and equal opportunities for placing questions on the agenda and for expressing reasons for endorsing one outcome rather than another. To deny any citizen adequate opportunities for effective participation means that because their preferences are unknown or incorrectly perceived, they cannot be taken into account.[1]

To deny people the right to participate is to deny them the right to have their voices heard. In 1776 Abigail Adams's entreaty to John to "remember the ladies" and not put unlimited power in the hands of men recognized that issues of concern to women would probably not receive consideration at the Continental Congress. The founders, imbued with English patriarchal tradition, believed that only those with a stake in the society were likely to be responsible citizens. Women (and unpropertied men) were too disorderly and were therefore at risk of exercising liberty without restraint. According to Mark Kann:

> The founders saw women as lustful, fickle, selfish creatures. The best way
> to limit women's mischief was to subordinate them to fathers and hus-
> bands and to focus their energies on bearing and nurturing children. The
> most dangerous and disorderly women were those who sought to escape
> domesticity for social pleasure and political action. These "public women"
> jeopardized their own well-being and their families' welfare but also social
> peace and order.[2]

This perspective manifested in the political structures and decision rules
created at the Constitutional Convention of 1787 (and the public policies
that came out of those structures and decision rules) and afterward rein-
forced the male patriarchy that dominated (and continues to dominate)
U.S. politics. The doors to participation and power were closed to women.
It wasn't until the suffragist movement of the nineteenth century that
women began to seek access to the political process and have their voices
heard. Since 1920, when women earned the right to participate and thus
have access to political power, women have gradually increased their participation in the political system. Although men and women are far from
equally represented as political actors, women have begun to reach parity
with men in political participation (and in some areas, such as voting, to
supercede them). Most of the dramatic changes in women's political participation have occurred in the past three decades.

All women citizens of voting age in the United States who meet other
eligibility criteria are guaranteed the right to vote in all elections by the
Nineteenth Amendment to the Constitution, ratified by the requisite number of states in August 1920. Before 1920 women could participate in politics in ways other than voting, and many did—for example, as part of the
women's suffrage movement. Ironically, many women did not vote in the
first few elections after 1920; either they believed politics was not women's
business, or their husbands opposed their participation. Women who came
of voting age after 1920 were more likely to vote than were their mothers.

We are no longer surprised by women as candidates and victors in congressional races, women as governors of states, or even women sitting as
justices on the Supreme Court. Since gaining the vote women have
opened the doors to power and now work where their voices can be
heard. Rather than having to ask men to "remember the ladies," women
now vote, run for office, and take on positions of responsibility in government. Indeed, a woman, Nancy Pelosi, is now the Democratic Leader of
the House of Representatives.

The story of four generations of women in the Lee family illustrates this evolution in women's political participation. Anna Lee did not vote in the 1920s because her husband, George, did not approve of women voting. However, Lee's daughter Barbara cast her first vote in the statewide election of 1920. Lee's granddaughter Carol became active in her political party's local organization in the 1940s. As a result of her continued work for the party, Carol was elected to the county party organization's executive committee and was later chosen as a delegate to the national party convention. Carol's daughter Donna, a schoolteacher, was elected to the local school board for two consecutive terms, after which she won a seat on the party's county council. When the incumbent state officeholder retired, she sought and won election to a statewide elective office. In four generations, the political participation of this family's women progressed from voting abstention to election to state office.

Women can now participate fully in political activities, but do they? Do men and women differ in their patterns of political activity? If so, how can these patterns of political activity be explained? This chapter and the next examine the changes in women's political participation that have occurred over the past three decades. This chapter explores patterns of participation in campaigns and elections, as well as in other types of political activity, by women who are not members of the political elite.[3] The term "political activity" as used here includes all types of action that attempt to influence, either directly or indirectly, what governments do: voting; contacting public officials; joining organizations that seek to influence executives, legislators, bureaucrats, and judges; and, less frequently, participating in strikes, boycotts, and protest demonstrations or marches. Activity intended to influence government policies also includes involvement in professional, social, or community organizations.

Americans are not particularly participative. In 1996 President Bill Clinton won reelection with the support of less than a quarter of eligible voters. In the 1988 congressional elections, considered to be a victory for the Democrats, only about 15 percent of eligible voters voted for Democratic candidates. With single-member districts as the cornerstone of our electoral system, a small number of voters (or nonvoters) can be incredibly influential. This became obvious in the presidential election of 2000 and has also occurred in such close races as the Sanchez/Dornan California congressional election in 1996, the McCloskey/McIntyre Indiana congressional race in 1984, and the Mack/MacKay Florida Senate race in 1988. When every vote counts, what are the differences between men and women in political participation? What factors affect women's participation in political activities?

PATTERNS OF POLITICAL PARTICIPATION

Changes in the life circumstances of most American women since the late 1970s have resulted in increased rates of political participation. More women are now employed outside the home. A larger proportion of women than men now attend college and obtain a degree. Both increased employment and more education are associated with increased political participation.[4] Those who participate are more likely to have the resources that facilitate participation—time, money, skills, and knowledge—and to have positive attitudes and beliefs about the value of participation in politics. Having these resources may make the individual more likely to participate voluntarily or to be willingly guided by others. For example, higher levels of education usually enhance the skills necessary for participation (reading comprehension, critical thinking, and so on) and lead to the acquisition of other resources, such as knowledge, verbal skills, and money or social status, which further facilitate participation. Thus cultural changes in education and employment have fostered changes in political participation.

Voting

When women finally gained the right to vote, their voter turnout rate was lower than expected and continued to be lower than that of men until 1980.[5] Voter turnout has been higher among women than among men in every presidential election since 1980 and continued to increase through the 2000 presidential election (see Table 5-1). From the presidential election of 1964 to the presidential election of 2000, the percentage difference in voter turnout has changed from a 4.9 percentage point advantage for men to a 3.1 percentage point advantage for women—an overall change of 8.0 percentage points. Scholars have uncovered similar patterns in congressional elections (see Table 5-2). From the congressional elections of 1966 to the congressional elections of 1998, the percentage difference in voter turnout has increased from a 5.2 point advantage for men to a 0.8 point advantage for women, an overall change of 6 percentage points. The percentage difference by race within each gender reporting

TABLE 5-1

Gender Differences in Voter Turnout in Presidential Elections, 1964–2000 (percent)

Year	Men	Women	Percentage difference
1964	71.9	67.0	−4.9
1968	69.8	66.0	−3.8
1972	64.1	62.0	−2.1
1976	59.6	58.8	−0.8
1980	59.1	59.4	+0.3
1984	59.0	60.8	+1.8
1988	56.4	58.3	+1.9
1992	60.2	62.3	+2.1
1996	52.8	55.5	+2.7
2000	53.1	56.2	+3.1

Source: U.S. Department of Commerce, Bureau of the Census, Current Population Reports, *Voting and Registration in the Election of November, 2000,* Series P-20-542, February 2002, Table C, www.census.gov/prod/2002pubs/ p20-542.pdf.

having voted in 2000 is 2.4 percentage points for whites (61.6 percent females to 59.2 percent males), 4.7 percentage points for Hispanics (29.8 percent females to 25.1 percent males), and 7.3 percentage points for blacks (57.3 percent females to 50 percent for males). Even if turnout rates were the same for both men and women, the fact that women outnumber men in the general voting age population would mean that more women than men would be voting in any particular election. Thus, in a national election, where the higher percentage of women voting than men is coupled with the fact that there are more women in the general voting age population than men, the difference between the number of men and women voters is in the millions. In 2000, for example, more than 7.5 million more women than men reported voting in the presidential election. The gender differences are even more pronounced when the voter's race is examined.[6]

Cheryl Christy examined change in voter turnout (and the variables believed to affect turnout) in the United States and other modern democracies over thirty-six years. She found a gradual decrease in gender differences in voter turnout rates.[7] Changes in social norms and electoral laws have eliminated or reduced several factors that once inhibited women's voting participation. To the extent that gender differences in voter turnout

TABLE 5-2

Gender Differences in Voter Turnout in Midterm Congressional
Elections, 1966–1998 (percent)

Year	Men	Women	Percentage difference
1966	58.2	53.0	−5.2
1970	56.8	52.7	−4.1
1974	46.3	43.4	−2.9
1978	46.6	45.3	−1.3
1982	48.7	48.4	−0.3
1986	45.8	46.1	+0.3
1990	44.6	45.4	+0.8
1994	44.7	45.3	+0.6
1998	41.4	42.2	+0.8

Source: U.S. Department of Commerce, Bureau of the Census, Current
Population Reports, *Voting and Registration in the Election of November, 1986,*
Series P-20, no. 414, Table A; *Voting and Registration in the Election of November,
1990,* Series P-20, no. 453, Table C. Data for 1994 were obtained from the
U.S. Census Bureau, www.census.gov/population/socdemo/voting/profile/
pttable1.dat. Data for 1998 were obtained from U.S. Department of Com-
merce, Bureau of the Census, Current Population Reports, *Voting and
Registration in the Election of November, 1998,* Series P-20-523 RV, Table A.

rates now exist, they tend to be affected by variables related to policy issues
and candidate characteristics, which vary from election to election.

Women's increased participation may also lead to changes in the
number of women among the political elite. Unfortunately some electoral
system factors depress the number of women in elite positions. Lane
Kenworthy and Melissa Malami explored inequality of gender representation in legislatures worldwide and discovered that the differences in electoral systems also played a significant role in gender inequality, with countries with single-member districts and first-past-the-post or plurality systems (only one winner and he or she gets the most votes, though not necessarily a majority) generally having fewer women in legislatures than
nations with multimember districts and proportional systems of voting
(where multiple representatives are elected in proportion to their votes
received in the election).[8]

In the United States, not only are women now more likely than men
to vote in presidential elections, but a gender gap is evident in party
choice.[9] A higher percentage of women than men have cast their votes for
Democratic candidates in presidential elections since 1980. In the 1996

presidential election, the gender gap helped Bill Clinton get reelected. While Clinton won the women's vote over Dole by a margin of 16 percentage points (54–38 percent), men supported Dole over Clinton by only 1 percentage point (44–43 percent). In the 2000 presidential race stronger male support for Bush over Gore (53–43 percent) counteracted women's support for Gore over Bush (54–42 percent). This pattern persists among voters of all age groups and education levels. In 2000, 44.1 percent of women thought of themselves as Democrats, whereas only 33.8 percent of men did. Conversely, 32.6 percent of men and 25.8 percent of women thought of themselves as Republicans. In Senate races in 2000, 57.3 percent of women voted for a Democratic candidate as compared with 46.9 percent of men. In congressional races in the same year, 55.2 percent of women voted for the Democratic candidate while 46.4 percent of men voted for the Democratic candidate. In congressional races in 2002, women's support of Republican candidates rose to 50 percent while men's support for Republican congressional candidates rose to 55 percent.

The gender gap is greatest among the most educated and the least educated voters. Differences among voters often reflects voters' perception of their economic self-interests. Differences also often reflect a greater awareness of the Democratic Party's support for equal opportunities for women and for government activism in solving problems related to social and educational policy. In 1992, for example, the major concern of women with less than a high school education was the economy and their children's economic future. College-educated women focused not only on the economy but also on the presidential candidates' positions on the abortion issue. This education-based gender gap appears to be growing. In the fall of 2003 a *USA Today*/CNN/Gallup Poll of more than 40,000 people discovered that there was a 10 percentage point gap between men and women with a high school degree or less who were leaning toward voting Democratic. The gap increased to 15 percentage points between men and women who had some college but had not graduated, to 20 percentage points between men and women with a college degree, and to 28 percentage points between men and women who had taken postgraduate courses. As the ranks of college-educated women continue to grow (another example of cultural change), will they have different policy preferences than less-educated women have?

Polls asking men and women to rank issues of importance to them also revealed differences between the sexes. In the fall of 2003 men ranked terrorism as the issue most important to them, followed in order by the economy, Iraq, education, and the deficit. Women ranked education first, then the economy, terrorism, Iraq, and Social Security. Political scientist John Hibbing concluded that although the state of the economy drives the voting behavior of both men and women, their standards for assessing the economy are different. According to Hibbing, "we found men tended to vote in terms of their personal economic situation, and women were more likely to vote on the nation's economic situation." [10] Will these differences persist or will the changing international scene, with its focus on terrorism and war, temper them? Will the "soccer moms" of the 1990s be replaced by the "security moms" of the twenty-first century?

Other Forms of Political Activity

In the 1960s women were less likely than men to engage in political activities other than voting. For example, in 1960 only college-educated women participated in political activity (defined as attending school board or city council meetings and contacting local officials) to the same extent as college-educated men. By 1976 women with a high school education were as likely to participate in these local activities as were men with a high school education.[11] By 1994 women were more likely than men to report having signed a petition. They were more likely than men to have attended a public meeting of a local government agency or school board, to have attended a political speech or rally, or to have written to a member of Congress or a state legislator.

Today women are also less likely than men to report participating in such campaign activities as working for a candidate or a party, contributing money, attending a political meeting or rally, trying to persuade someone else how to vote, and wearing a campaign button or displaying a campaign sticker. One reason why people participate in politics is because someone asks them to. In 2000, 38 percent of men and 37.6 percent of women reported being contacted by someone from a political party. Men are more likely to be asked to give money than are women. In 1992 men were contacted more frequently than women, both in person and by phone and mail, with requests to make campaign contributions. As a consequence, men were more likely than women to report making contributions.[12] In 2000 men were more likely to contribute to a candidate (8.8 percent of men as compared with 5 percent of women) and also more likely to contribute to a political party (9.1 percent of men as compared with 4.3 percent of women).[13]

Beginning in the 1980s, several groups affiliated with each of the two major parties made valiant efforts to increase women's campaign contributions—especially those to women candidates. These organizations focus on candidates for the House of Representatives and the Senate as well as on candidates for major statewide and local offices. Two of the most prominent such organizations are EMILY's List (an acronym for Early Money Is Like Yeast), which supports Democratic candidates, and the Wish List, which supports Republican candidates. Other groups are affiliated with a professional association, such as the political action committee (PAC) associated with the American Nurses Association. The number of PACs focusing on women candidates at the federal level shot up during the last quarter of the twentieth century. In 1976 only four such PACs existed; in 1992 forty-five registered with the Federal Election Commission and twenty-nine made contributions to women candidates for federal office.[14] In 1996 fifty-five PACs and donor networks either supported mostly women candidates or raised money primarily by soliciting contributions from women. Nine of those groups operated at the national level; thirty-seven focused on particular states.[15] By 2003 the number of PACs and donor networks contributing money primarily to women candidates had declined to forty-two (thirteen national PACs and twenty-nine state or local PAC networks).[16]

These women's PACs have significantly increased the amount of money that women give to political candidates. Women's PACs contributed $11.5 million to women candidates for office in 1992, compared with $1.1 million in 1988. Their support also increases the ability of women candidates to raise sufficient funds to be competitive in contests for local, state, and national offices.[17] Several studies conclude that, after taking into account the type of contest (open seat as compared with incumbent challenger) and the partisan nature of the district, women are not disadvantaged in raising funds to run for the House of Representatives.[18] Other research on local elections suggests that women are more likely to give to women candidates than to men candidates.[19] A study by the Center for Responsive Politics of campaign differences through the 1990s provides further clarification of gender differences in campaign contributions. In the 1997–1998 election cycle women accounted for 24.5 percent of all hard money contributions to candidates, parties, and PACs and 12.2 percent of soft money contributions. Although women contributed at higher rates to Democratic candidates than their male counterparts in both hard money (50.4 percent to 41.9 percent) and soft money (61.4 percent to 46.5 percent) in the

1997–1998 election cycle, the overall percentage rate for women declined over the decade for both hard money contributions (from 26.4 percent in 1991–1992 to 24.5 percent in 1997–1998) and soft money contributions (from 14.1 percent in 1991–1992 to 12.2 percent in 1997–1998). The study also discovered that in the 1998 congressional elections, female Democratic candidates were the most likely to have women contributing to their campaigns. Forty-three percent of contributions over $200 received by Democratic women candidates came from women. Women gave 29.4 percent of the same contributions for Republican women candidates, 25.8 percent for Democratic male candidates, and 23.8 percent for Republican male candidates. The study also discovered that the gender gap in party voting is a function of the increasing support of Republican candidates by men.[20]

Focusing on explicitly political activity may ignore important forms of participation in community activities, which provide an opportunity to develop leadership and communications skills that can be used in politics. Community activities may also serve as a means to acquire politically relevant information and to facilitate informal communication with community leaders. A longitudinal study of Americans who were first interviewed as high school seniors in 1972 provides evidence of different patterns of community and political participation among men and women. When interviewed in 1972, the women were more likely to be active in and assume a leadership role in high school activities than were the men. When these members of the "baby boomer" generation were interviewed again in 1986, significant gender differences appeared in membership in community organizations. Men were significantly more likely to be members of union, farm, and professional organizations; sports teams or clubs; and service organizations. Women were more likely to be members of youth, religious, and educational or academic organizations. When we consider the total number of activities in which each of these baby boomers was a member, we find that women were slightly more likely to be members of, and active participants in, community organizations.[21]

But community activities and membership in organizations did not translate into political participation. Men were more likely than women to report trying to persuade others to vote for a particular candidate, to contribute money to campaigns, to attend political gatherings, and to have held political or governmental office. Men were also more likely to report sometimes or frequently talking about political problems with friends, coworkers, community leaders, and elected officials.[22]

A national survey conducted in 1990 that focused on political participation provides additional evidence that women are less politically active
than men. Women were less likely to contribute to political campaigns, to
work informally in the community, to serve on a local governing board,
to contact a government official, or to be affiliated with a political organization. When the eight possible types of political participation are combined to obtain an index of participation ranging from zero to eight,
women are found to have a lower average political participation score
than men.[23]

To what extent are women willing to engage in less conventional forms
of political participation? A 1974 study reports that women of all age
groups are less supportive than men of unconventional political action such
as participating in a protest.[24] Data from other studies confirm this finding
and suggest that support for protest activities is a function of the social and
political context. During the Vietnam War (1968–1974), disapproval of
protest meetings, sit-ins, and antiwar demonstrations decreased as the war
became more unpopular. The proportion of men disapproving of protest
activities decreased from 74 percent in 1968 to 62 percent in 1974; the
proportion of women disapproving decreased from 77 percent in 1968 to
59 percent in 1974.[25]

EXPLANATIONS FOR PATTERNS OF POLITICAL PARTICIPATION

A person's political participation is influenced by his or her resources,
social status, motivation to participate, and the legal structure and political environment.[26] All of these factors are intertwined and have changed
remarkably in the past three decades. The expansion of opportunities for
women in education and occupation along with attendant changes in
the legal and political environment have increased women's social status,
their motivation to participate, their resources, and their success (which is
explored in the next chapter). Resources that facilitate participation
include both education and life experiences. Social status may be con-
ferred by personal achievement or by group membership (in social,
service, and religious organizations). Certain attitudes, such as a sense
of moral obligation to participate in politics, an empowering sense of
personal political efficacy, loyal commitment to a candidate or political
party, concern about a policy issue or set of issues, and the social context

(including pressures to participate that may exist in any social status group) may stimulate both social and political involvement—that is, interest in and attention to politics and public policy and concern with the outcome of political processes. Individuals may also be motivated by candidates, political parties, social and political movements, and interest groups. Participation in elections may be increased or decreased by voter eligibility requirements and by the administrative processes, such as voter registration, that regulate the electoral process. The political environment also affects patterns of participation. For example, in some localities women are encouraged to be candidates for elective office, whereas in others, local political elites discourage women from running for office.

Differences in people's education partly explain both historical and current patterns of political participation. Those with more education generally know more about the political system and have a better understanding of how government policies affect their lives. They are also more likely to believe that political activities can change policy outcomes. Peer pressure to participate is generally greater in the social environment of such individuals. Social norms in both the parental family and the adult peer group contribute to the pressure to participate, at least in voting. Education also enables people to acquire, process, and analyze information that helps them make judgments about courses of political action.[27] Those with more education are also likely to have more skill in dealing with bureaucracies, which was a necessary part of voter registration prior to the implementation in 1995 of the federal "motor voter" law, which has made registration much more accessible.[28] Experiences in educational institutions or religious institutions and social or service clubs can lead people to acquire the resources and skills necessary for more demanding forms of political activity, such as working for a political party or with an interest group, or running for office.[29]

Type of employment also influences political participation, and as educational and occupational opportunities continue to increase for women their political participation should increase too. Women who work outside the home may have greater exposure to information about how government policies affect their interests and may feel pressure from coworkers or employers to participate. Women in the work force may also more directly experience the effects of federal, state, and local government policies requiring nondiscrimination in education, employment, training, and promotion.[30]

TABLE 5-3

Gender Differences in Political Involvement, Presidential Elections, 1952–2000 (percent)

Year	Interested in the campaign		Care a good deal who wins the election		Follow politics some or most of the time	
	Men	Women	Men	Women	Men	Women
1952	40	34	69	65	—	—
1956	34	26	66	61	—	—
1960	42	34	68	63	71	54
1964	40	36	66	66	70	66
1968	44	35	66	64	71	58
1972	37	27	61	60	80	68
1976	41	34	58	56	78	64
1980	33	27	56	56	69	55
1984	33	25	66	64	68	59
1988	32	25	64	59	69	52
1992	42	36	76	76	74	62
1996	22	24	78	80	72	56
2000	21	23	79	76	71	50

Source: Calculated from data in University of Michigan, Center for Political Studies, "1952–1990 American National Election Studies Cumulative File" and the 1992, 1996, and 2000 American National Election Studies.

Note: The "follow politics" question was not asked in 1952 or 1956.

Men are more likely than women to report that they follow what is going on in politics, care a good deal about who wins elections, and are interested in campaigns (see Table 5-3). Men have a higher participation rate than women in political campaigns. One explanation may be men's higher level of political involvement in general or their interest in and attention to what happens in government and politics. In 2000 men were still more likely than women to discuss politics with family and friends (82.9 percent versus 79.3 percent) and to try to convince someone to vote a certain way (39.9 percent versus 31.4 percent).[31] Despite this gender difference, women are now more likely than men to vote. However, women are less likely to participate in campaigns and in some other types of political activity, such as contacting public officials.

A commitment to a political party and concern with its success in help-ing candidates get elected to office can motivate someone to become involved in politics. One measure of this commitment is strength of party identification. The expectation is that those who more strongly identify themselves as a party member will be more likely to vote and to partici-pate in campaigns. Women do not differ significantly from men in strength of party identification. However, as previously mentioned, women are more likely than men to identify with the Democratic Party.

Political attitudes and beliefs affect political participation. People who believe that they can be politically effective and that the government is responsive to voters' concerns are more likely to participate by voting and participating in campaigns. A person who shares this belief may also believe that public officials care about his or her opinions—a measure of external political efficacy. In 2000 women were less likely to have this perception, which reflects past patterns of public policy in which women's concerns and policy needs received less attention from (mostly male) public offi-cials.[32] Internal political efficacy includes a belief that politics and govern-ment are not too complicated to understand, as well as confidence that one understands the important national issues and is well qualified to partici-pate in politics. In 2000 women as a group were found to feel less internal political efficacy than men.[33]

The resources and opportunities to participate also vary with individu-als' social circumstances. One crucial resource is time. Voting turnout among men does not vary with the number of children in the household. In contrast, the more children in the household, the less likely women are to vote. Women are less likely than men to work outside the home; women who do tend to be employed in jobs that do not facilitate the acquisition or exercise of politically relevant skills. Furthermore, women's incomes tend to be lower; in a two-income family, the proportion contributed by the woman tends to be less. Women's participation in religious and volun-tary organizations constitutes an alternative resource for political participa-tion (by facilitating the development of participatory skills) that partially offsets the advantages accruing to men as a result of their higher education and income and their advantage in terms of job skills.[34]

Taking advantage of unusual alternatives has been a theme in women's political participation. When Abigail Adams's entreaty of John to "remem-ber the ladies" was largely ignored, women found other ways to contribute to civic life. At the turn of the past century suffragists began to pry open the door to political participation for women. By the 1970s economic and social opportunities for women were expanding. Although women are somewhat less likely to participate in many activities associated with politics, women now vote at higher rates than men. We should expect to see more and more women among the political elite—the subject of the next chapter. Thus, when women now say that a woman's place is in the house— they may be referring to the House of Representatives!

SUGGESTIONS FOR FURTHER READING

In Print

Carty, Linda, ed. 1993. *And Still We Rise: Feminist Political Mobilizing in Contemporary Canada.* Toronto: Women's Press.

Darcy, Robert E., Charles D. Hadley, and Jason F. Kirksey. 1993. "Election Systems and the Representation of Black Women in American State Legislatures." *Women and Politics* 13, no. 2: 73–89.

Herrick, Rebekah. 1996. "Is There a Gender Gap in the Value of Campaign Resources?" *American Politics Quarterly* 24, no. 1 (January): 68–80.

Lockwood, Victoria S. 1993. *Tahitian Transformation: Gender and Capitalist Development in a Rural Society.* Boulder, Colo.: Lynne Rienner.

Lorber, Judith, and Farrell, Susan A., eds. 1991. *The Social Construction of Gender.* Newbury Park, Calif.: Sage Publications.

Rapoport, Ronald, Walter Stone, and Alan Abramowitz. 1991. "Sex and the Caucus Participant: The Gender Gap and Presidential Nominations." *American Journal of Political Science* 515 (May): 23–37.

Rusciano, Frank Louis. 1992. "Rethinking the Gender Gap: The Case of West German Elections, 1949–1987." *Comparative Politics* 24, no. 3 (April): 335–357.

Schubert, Glendon A. 1991. *Sexual Politics and Political Feminism.* Greenwich, Conn.: JAI Press.

Small, Lisa. 1992. "Presidential Campaign Ignores Women's Issues." *New Directions for Women* 21, no. 3 (May–June): 3.

On the Web

Center for American Women and Politics. *www.rci.rutgers.edu/~cawp.* The center is a unit of the Eagleton Institute of Politics at Rutgers, The State University of New Jersey. This Web site provides a vast array of information about the status and prospects of women in government and politics at all levels.

The Center for Responsive Politics. *www.opensecrets.org.* The Center for Responsive Politics is a nonpartisan, nonprofit research group that explores the role of money in U.S. politics, especially its effect on elections and public policy. The center's objectives are to create a more educated voter, an involved citizenry, and a more responsive government.

League of Women Voters. *www.lwv.org.* Carrie Chapman Catt founded this organization in 1920 during the convention of the National American Woman Suffrage Association. Its original mission was to help women carry out their new responsibilities as voters. Today the League's mission is to encourage informed and active citizen participation in government, to increase understanding of major public policy issues, and to influence public policy through education and advocacy.

National Election Studies. *www.umich.edu/~nes/.* The National Election Studies produce high-quality data on voting, public opinion, and political participation for social scientists, teachers, students, policy makers, and journalists.

NOTES

1. Robert Dahl, *Democracy and Its Critics* (New Haven: Yale University Press, 1989), 109.

2. Mark E. Kann, *The Gendering of American Politics* (Westport, Conn.: Praeger Publishers, 1999), 3.

3. "Political elite" refers collectively to persons holding an elective or appointive office in a local or state government or in the federal government.

4. See Sandra Baxter and Marjorie Lansing, *Women and Politics: The Invisible Majority* (Ann Arbor: University of Michigan Press, 1980); Karen Beckwith, *American Women and Political Participation* (New York: Greenwood Press, 1986); M. Margaret Conway, *Political Participation in the United States,* 3d ed. (Washington, D.C.: CQ Press, 2000); Raymond E. Wolfinger and Steven J. Rosenstone, *Who Votes?* (New Haven: Yale University Press, 1980); Steven J. Rosenstone and John Mark Hansen, *Mobilization, Participation, and Democracy in America* (New York: Macmillan, 1993); and Ruy A. Teixeira, *The Disappearing American Voter* (Washington, D.C.: Brookings Institution, 1992).

5. Martin Gruberg, *Women in American Politics* (Oshkosh, Wis.: Academica Press, 1968), 9.

6. Center for American Women and Politics, *Sex Differences in Voter Turnout,* fact sheet (New Brunswick, N.J.: Eagleton Institute of Politics, Rutgers University, 2002).

7. Cheryl Christy, "Trends in Sex Differences in Political Participation: A Comparative Perspective," in Marianne Githens, Pippa Norris, and Joni Lovenduski, eds., *Different Voices, Different Roles* (New York: HarperCollins, 1994), 27–37.

8. Lane Kenworthy and Melissa Malami, "Gender Inequality and Political Representation: A Worldwide Comparative Analysis," *Social Forces* 78 (1999): 237.

9. See Sue Tolleson-Rinehart and Kenneth Hanses, "Gendered Parties, Partisan Gender Roles: The Four Groups Who Cause the Gender Gap, 1980–1988" (paper presented at the meeting of the Midwest Political Science Association, Chicago, 1992); Mary E. Bendyna and Celinda C. Lake, "Gender and Voting in the 1992 Presidential Election," in Elizabeth Adell Cook, Sue Thomas, and Clyde Wilcox, *The Year of the Woman: Myths and Realities* (Boulder, Colo.: Westview Press, 1994), 236–254. See also Carole Chaney and Barbara Sinclair, "Women and the 1992 House Elections," in Cook, Thomas, and Wilcox, *Year of the Woman,* 123–139.

10. "Til Politics Do Us Part: Gender Gap Widens," *USA Today,* December 18, 2003, 1–2.

11. Nancy McGlen and Karen O'Connor, *Women's Rights* (New York: Praeger, 1983), 105–106.

12. Calculated from data in University of Michigan, Center for Political Studies, "1992 American National Election Study." In 1992, 8.9 percent of the men reported making a political contribution, compared with 5.6 percent of women. The difference is statistically significant ($p = 0.0064$).

13. Calculated from data in University of Michigan, Center for Political Studies, "2000 American National Election Study," variables 1229 and 1231.

14. Susan Roberts, "Furthering Feminism and Female Representation: The Role of Women's PACs in Recruitment" (paper presented at the meeting of the Midwest Political Science Association, Chicago, 1993). In 1992 forty-two political action committees either gave money predominantly to women or had a donor base composed largely of women.

15. Center for American Women and Politics, "Women's PACs in 1990: Continuing to Make a Difference," *News and Notes* 9 (1993): 10; and 10 (winter 1996): 6; cited in Chaney and Sinclair, "Women and the 1992 House Elections," 130.

16. Center for American Women and Politics, "Women's PACs and Donor Networks: A Contact List," fact sheet (New Brunswick, N.J.: Eagleton Institute of Politics, Rutgers University, 2003).

17. Candice J. Nelson, "Women's PACs in the Year of the Woman," in Cook, Thomas, and Wilcox, *Year of the Woman,* 181–195.

18. Chaney and Sinclair, "Women and the 1992 House Elections," 128; Barbara Burrell, *A Woman's Place Is in the House* (Ann Arbor: University of Michigan Press, 1994), chap. 6; Joanne Marie Connor, "Dynamics of Open Seat Elections for the United States House of Representatives" (Ph.D. diss., University of Florida, 1994); and Carole J. Uhlaner and Kay Lehman Schlozman, "Candidate Gender and Congressional Campaign Receipts," *Journal of Politics* 48 (1984): 30–50.

19. Gerald Ingalls and Theodore S. Arrington, "The Role of Gender in Local Campaign Financing: The Case of Charlotte, North Carolina," *Women and Politics* 11 (1991): 61–89.

20. Center for Responsive Politics, "Sex, Money and Politics: The Gender Gap in Campaign Contributions," 2004, www.opensecrets.org/pubs/gender/index.asp.

21. Calculated from data in U.S. Department of Education, Office of Educational Research and Improvement, "National Longitudinal Study of the High School Class of 1972" (Washington, D.C.: National Center for Educational Statistics, n.d.).

22. Ibid.

23. Kay Lehman Schlozman, Nancy Burns, and Sidney Verba, "Gender and Pathways to Participation: The Role of Resources," *Journal of Politics* 56 (November 1994): 963–990.

24. Alan Marsh and Max Kaase, "Background of Political Action," in Samuel H. Barnes and Max Kaase, *Political Action* (Beverly Hills, Calif.: Sage Publications, 1979), Table 4.2, 108.

25. Calculated from data in University of Michigan, Center for Political Studies, "1952–1990 American National Election Studies Cumulative File," variable 642.

26. Sidney Verba, Kay Lehman Schlozman, and Henry E. Brady, *Voice and Equality* (Cambridge: Harvard University Press, 1995).

27. See Gabriel Almond and Sidney Verba, *The Civic Culture* (Princeton: Princeton University Press, 1963), 379–381; Wolfinger and Rosenstone, *Who Votes?* chap. 2; and Conway, *Political Participation in the United States,* 25–29.

28. The "motor voter" law requires all states to make voter registration forms available in state agencies such as the motor vehicle registration bureaus and drivers' licensing agencies. Congress enacted the national voter registration bill in May 1993; the law went into effect January 1, 1995.

29. Verba, Schlozman, and Brady, *Voice and Equality,* chap. 11.

30. See M. Margaret Conway, David W. Ahern, and Gertrude A. Steuernagel, *Women and Public Policy: A Revolution in Progress,* 2d ed. (Washington, D.C.: CQ Press, 1999), chap. 4.

31. Calculated from data in University of Michigan, Center for Political Studies, "2000 American National Election Studies File."

32. Calculated from data in University of Michigan, Center for Political Studies, "2000 American National Election Study." For a discussion of the policy needs of women, see Conway, Ahern, and Steuernagel, *Women and Public Policy.*

33. Calculated from data in University of Michigan, Center for Political Studies, "2000 American National Election Study."

34. Schlozman, Burns, and Verba, "Gender and Pathways to Participation," Table 5, 984.

CHAPTER 6

Opening the Doors to Political Power:
Women as Members of the Political Elite

In 2002 Mary L. Landrieu was reelected to the U.S. Senate from Louisiana. In 1996 she had become the first woman from that state to be elected to a full term in the Senate. Landrieu was the daughter of Moon Landrieu, former mayor of New Orleans and U. S. secretary of Housing and Urban Development, and part of a family with a long history of public service. Her first political office was a seat in the Louisiana House of Representatives in 1979. She was the youngest woman ever elected to the state legislature, and she advocated for children and families. In 1987 she successfully ran for Louisiana state treasurer.

As one of fourteen women in the U.S. Senate, today Mary Landrieu is on powerful committees such as Appropriations, Armed Services, Energy and Natural Resources, and Small Business. She also serves on several appropriations subcommittees, including Agriculture, Labor, Health and Education, and Military Construction. Landrieu is an example of the dramatic and fundamental change that has occurred in women's political participation since the 1970s. Most party politicians at that time viewed women as party cheerleaders and campaign workers who performed secretarial work—stuffing envelopes, licking stamps, and distributing campaign literature—but who should not be involved in strategic political decisions. As Landrieu's father put it, "women do the lickin' and the stickin' while men plan the strategy." Susan and Martin Tolchin concluded that

> The very texture of American politics—its folkways and byways—militates
> against women's entry into the mainstream. The smoke-filled rooms, bour-
> bon and branchwater rites, and all-night poker games exclude women
> from the fellowship and cronyism that seals the bonds of power. It is an
> exclusion practiced by Republicans and Democrats, reformers and regu-
> lars, liberals and conservatives. It crosses economic and social barriers,
> showing little distinction between rich and poor, social lions, the upwardly
> mobile, and the disinherited. Nor do years of service, party loyalty, wis-
> dom, or experience provide women with a passport to those inner circles
> where priorities are set, careers advanced, and strategies determined.

Thirty years ago, America's political culture, "its folkways and byways,"
excluded women from power. The late New Jersey state legislator
Millicent Fenwick once commented, "Women are on the outside when
the door to the smoke-filled room is closed."[1] In other words, women's
work for parties and for candidates was not translating into more appointments to positions of influence.

On October 8, 1991, a door again became a symbol of the obstacles
that women had to overcome—this time to gain access to a room in the
powerful U.S. Senate. Barbara Boxer, elected senator from California in
1992, has discussed a defining moment in the mobilization of women—
the possibility that they would be denied participation in a Senate decision on whether to pursue extensive questioning of Supreme Court nom-
inee Clarence Thomas. Thomas had been accused of sexual harassment by
University of Oklahoma law professor Anita Hill. Two days after Hill
made the allegations, when it appeared that both the House and Senate
were unwilling to thoroughly explore the charges, representatives Patricia
Schroeder, D–Colo.; Barbara Boxer, D–Calif.; Eleanor Holmes Norton,
D–D.C.; Louise Slaughter, D–N.Y.; Jolene Unsoeld, D–Wash.; Nita
Lowey, D–N.Y.; and Patsy Mink, D–Hawaii, walked out of the House of
Representatives and over to the Senate. Reporters and photographers followed; the photograph of the seven women marching up the steps of the
Senate has been described as "the women's Iwo Jima"—a comparison to
the raising of the U.S. flag on the Pacific island during World War II. This
action, captured in this photo, made an indelible mark on the public consciousness and came to symbolize something far more profound than the
event itself.

Boxer explained the women's feelings:

> As often happens when people act in synch, there was little talking as we walked. We didn't plan what we would tell the senators but we knew that we'd tell them the truth about what we were feeling. And we knew that we would be of help to them—and we wanted to be of help; with only two women in the Senate, they could use our perspective. We felt that we would be welcome, or that at least our advice would be welcome.

The women went to the room in the Senate where the members of the Democratic caucus were discussing the Thomas nomination, knocked on the door, and were told by a senior congressional aide that they could not come in. They told a female staffer that the reporters who had accompanied them knew why they had come and would certainly be interested to know the outcome. After some delay, the staffer told them that the Senate majority leader would see them in the side room. Boxer has reflected on these events:

> The day we knocked on that door was an extraordinary circumstance, as history has shown. The seven of us were the only group of women in the country who could get at all close to where the decision over Clarence Thomas would be made. It's hard for me to explain how it felt for seven grown women, experienced in life and in politics, to have to pound on a closed door, to have to beg to be heard on a crucial issue that couldn't really wait for niceties.

A senator later told Boxer that strangers were not allowed in that room; strangers in this context meant people who were not senators. But for Boxer, "the truth is that women have been strangers in the Senate . . . strangers in the highest, most powerful legislative body in the world."[2]

Boxer's story aids in understanding the U.S. political system, contemporary political culture, and the changing role that women have in U.S. politics. Women are still underrepresented in the halls of power, but they are beginning to make a difference. Although those seven women were unable to stop the selection of Clarence Thomas, they raised public consciousness about sexual harassment. The Senate committee, political commentators, and the general public had shown an ignorance of sexual harassment that incensed many women and spurred them to vote in 1992. This large turnout helped to unseat an incumbent president and increase nearly twofold the number of women in Congress.

Since the mid-1960s women have organized caucuses and interest groups such as the National Organization for Women, the National Women's Political Caucus, EMILY's List (Early Money Is Like Yeast), and the Congressional Caucus for Women's Issues to lobby for women's concerns, to encourage women to seek elective office, and to support women candidates. And women have become increasingly visible as political actors; no longer merely "cheerleaders," they now seek and win elective office and are appointed to positions of power and responsibility in political organizations at all levels (local, state, and national) and in all three branches of government (legislative, executive, and judicial).

Most of the success stories in this chapter date from 1973; however, women enjoyed some success before the 1970s. Women's participation in and leadership of the dominant social movements of the nineteenth century shaped public policy, resulting in improved working conditions, more educational opportunities, and passage of the Thirteenth and Nineteenth Amendments. Many of these social movements provided women the opportunity to be leaders in ways denied to them in the traditional institutions of political power. Women today are active in similar social movements. The changes that have occurred in women's political attitudes and political participation were the subject of previous chapters. This chapter explores women's recent successes in opening the doors to higher levels of political power and becoming members of the political elite.

WOMEN, POWER, AND THE POLITICAL CULTURE

The small group of people who hold high-level positions of power and responsibility in a government is generally called the political elite. They help shape political values and control government resources, thereby influencing the politics of the society. Throughout most of U.S. history, women have not been members of the political elite; therefore, the issues of importance to women have been either absent from or at the bottom of the public agenda. Women's more recent advances in gaining political representation (although certainly not in proportion to their numbers) have come despite the fact that the political system largely reflects the values of affluent white males. As women increasingly assume leadership positions in political organizations such as the major political parties, they will have an opportunity to change how these institutions operate (as did Barbara

Boxer and her six colleagues) and to influence public policies, thus ultimately influencing the political culture. Women's ability to lead within these organizations and institutions can have dramatic consequences for women specifically and for society in general. Now is the time to ask two questions: What is leadership? How will society's view of leadership affect women's political future?

Gendered Notions of Leadership

Women's long absence from positions of political power has conditioned society to associate the characteristics of leadership with male behavior. Two frequently cited definitions of politics reflect a male orientation: politics is about "who gets what, where, when, why and how," and politics is about "the authoritative allocation of values for society"—that is, capturing resources and redistributing them from losers to winners. Is that what politics is really about? Many observers, such as Nel Noddings, assert that this is clearly a male approach. Perhaps if more women had been leaders throughout history, leadership might be associated with the ability to get individuals and groups to work together to find a common ground. Is the ability to get people to do something (in other words, to exert power over them) a better definition of leadership than one that emphasizes the ability to get people to reason together and to seek compromise (in other words, to empower them)? Is there any theory that logically and convincingly equates the use of power or force with leadership, or is this simply the male standard? Noddings argues that creating a more egalitarian educational system requires a long-term effort to challenge the male standard that is dominant in education and to replace it with a female standard.[3] In other words, Noddings argues that changes in the nature of education will, over time, lead to cultural change regarding society's view of leadership.

The influence of the male standard was evident in some political pundits' assessments of President Bill Clinton and Hillary Rodham Clinton. Bill Clinton was often criticized for taking too long to make a decision, listening to too many viewpoints, and changing his mind several times before reaching a decision. More manly and presidential would have been making a decision and sticking with it, choosing a point of view and then fighting for it. Hillary Rodham Clinton was and still is criticized from the opposite perspective as being too strong, too power hungry. Political pundits use derogatory titles such as "the Iron Lady," and bumper stickers during the Clinton presidency proclaimed "I didn't vote for President Hillary" or "Impeach Clinton (and Her Husband, Too)." Someone who is "made of iron" is considered to be strong or tough, and toughness is a desired attribute in a man but not a woman.

"Leadership" has no universally accepted definition. Richard Neustadt, one of the most respected scholars of the American presidency, asserts that presidential power is the power to persuade, and the power to persuade is the ability to bargain.[4] Although persuasion is an important mechanism for exerting power and influence, this definition of presidential power does not imply the use of force. Camilla Stivers observes that there have been hundreds of attempts to define the term "leadership," and that the vagueness of the term and the continued reliance on the term are ideological in two ways. "Leadership is an important cultural myth by which we make sense of and impart significance to organizational and political experience; in addition, leadership is an idea used to support and rationalize the continuation of existing political-economic, racial, and gender arrangements."[5] Her insightful comments may explain the difficulties some women encounter when being evaluated for positions of leadership. A strong leader, whether in business, the military, or politics, attempts to exert his or her will over a situation. This conditions how the public will rate the capabilities of other aspiring leaders. Well-to-do white males have been the titans of business and the military; many of them have argued that, on the basis of these credentials, they should hold the reins of political power as well. If this view continues to prevail, of course, it will ensure the continued domination of society by a wealthy white patriarchy. The changes in the educational and career opportunities available to women over the past thirty-plus years, however, indicate that public attitudes have changed and probably will continue to do so. Women, however, need to be vigilant to make sure they have access to all of the organizations and institutions (educational, business, and social) that enable them to display leadership traits.

Women's Political Future

Today's political environment—shaped by the 2001 terrorist attacks on the World Trade Center, ongoing military actions in Afghanistan and Iraq, and the 2004 presidential campaign—threaten to reinforce the male standard of leadership. The political issues likely to dominate the presidential election are the fight against terrorism, the decision to go to war in Iraq, and the military service of the incumbent president and his Democratic challenger. Part of the dialogue during the presidential campaign will surely focus on who has the characteristics necessary to lead the fight against terrorism. Will these issues reinforce the male standard of leadership? In a January 29, 2004, opinion piece, written after the New Hampshire primary, entitled "The Politics of Manliness," conservative political columnist George Will stated:

> New Hampshire confirmed what Iowa intimated. Democrats who are serious about the candidates' electability understand that seriousness requires a retreat from the feminization of politics. . . . And the Democrats' movement away from feminization explains John Kerry's brisk forward march, with a military cadence. . . . Kerry's "patrician aloofness" may be manly reticence. But he has embraced today's confessional ethos by making autobiography serve as political philosophy and reducing his narrative to a war story. Riding his Harley, gunning for Iowa pheasants, and playing hockey in New Hampshire have expressed his campaign's subtext: manliness.

Feminized politics, according to Carnes Lord of the Naval War College, justifies all policies with reference to their impact on children. In his book *The Modern Prince: What Leaders Need to Know Now,* Lord says leadership is a problematic concept in today's democracies. Modern technology has produced prosperity, which has produced a middle class growing in size, competence (education), security (homeownership, 401(k)s, etc.) and self-confidence (assertion of rights). All this, plus the egalitarian, antihierarchical spirit of the age, plus the rarity of great wars, threatens to make politics seem unimportant and leaders seem dispensable.

Leadership, Lord says, presupposes some element of "such traditionally manly qualities as competitiveness, aggression or, for that matter, the ability to command." Because "leadership that is not prepared to disadvantage anyone is hardly leadership at all."[6]

Is George Will correct? Does the context of today's politics encourage a withdrawal from the "feminization" of politics? Will issues of importance to women and women's leadership style be overshadowed by terrorism and war? Domestic issues such as health care, education, social security, and economic opportunity could fade into the background as the presidential candidates try to reinforce their military leadership credentials. Although this will probably not affect women candidates at state and local levels, will it affect women's chances in future national races? Are people asking, "Can women lead during times of conflict?" In other countries at other times women have lead their countries through war: Golda Meir in Israel during the Yom Kippur War and Margaret Thatcher in Britain during the Falklands conflict.

If the male standard continues to predominate in American political culture, the likelihood that women will ever attain positions of leadership in
proportion to their numbers is uncertain. Women will always start off at a
disadvantage when competing with men, and they will have to win in spite
of their gender. Society's consciousness of the different approaches to leadership needs to be raised, and indeed it can be raised as society learns more
about women's leadership in organizations and social movements. Women
are still underrepresented at the top levels of major corporations; however,
many have become successful entrepreneurs, managing their own small
and medium-size businesses. Women's success in the political arena and the
continued entry of women into the political elite are key to changing society's attitude toward leadership and women's perception of their own abilities as political leaders. Women who have attained positions of leadership
and responsibility in political organizations and institutions are role models for others, demonstrating (to society as well) the leadership skills that
women have to offer.

WOMEN'S POLITICAL PARTICIPATION: A CLOSER LOOK

Women's success in gaining formal access to the halls of power is a relatively recent phenomenon, but women have pursued diverse social policy
objectives for more than two centuries. Feminist scholars such as Glenna
Matthews have only recently begun to document the important role that
women have played in shaping public policy.[7] These works provide a clear-
er picture of American society, past and present. They extol women's contributions and encourage women to participate at higher levels of political
organizations and government institutions. In this section we explore the
history of what Matthews calls "the rise of public woman."

Women's Political Involvement, 1840–1970

As mentioned earlier, women were influencing the policy process even
before they gained the right to vote. Why, then, has the image of the apo-
litical woman prevailed? The responsibility must lie at least partly with
political science. Influenced by traditional notions of appropriate sex-role
behavior, many scholars fostered a perception of politics as a "man's game."
They did not think of women's involvement in reform movements as

being political; rather, they argued that women's interest in child care, health, and education followed naturally from their role as nurturers, and that women's involvement in causes such as prohibition and abolition were appropriate for them as guardians of the nation's morality.

Feminist scholars have challenged this perception, arguing that these activities constituted political participation. They point out that even before the Civil War, when women were excluded from voting and holding public office, they spoke out publicly against slavery and participated in the Underground Railroad. Women educated the children of slaves, an action that violated many state laws and could have had serious political consequences. Women were also part of the labor movement in the United States in the 1840s. As the nation industrialized a need arose for groups that would give voice to workers' concerns; women played key roles in helping achieve humane conditions in U.S. factories.

Winning the right to vote was the beginning of the political empowerment of women. According to Glenna Matthews, the successes of the women's suffrage movement affected women's later efforts in two ways. First, the parades and protests staged by the suffrage movement made many women realize the value of using ritualized public behavior to pursue women's interests. Such demonstrations proved to women that rather than relying on sympathetic men to advance women's causes and interests (as Abigail Adams did when she asked John to "remember the ladies"), women could act for themselves. Second, women recognized that intense politicking of officeholders and important members of political parties was a valuable tactic. Matthews observes that nineteenth century middle-class women were expected to be high-minded and to maintain decorum, but

> Following the failure of the Reconstruction Amendments to enfranchise women, [Elizabeth Cady] Stanton and [Susan B.] Anthony had begun to push in a somewhat different direction, willing to anger their opponents, for example, as they demanded justice for women. Under [Carrie Chapman] Catt's tutelage, women began to operate in a fashion that was forceful without being confrontational. . . . Catt personally lobbied Woodrow Wilson, asking him for advice and trying to associate him with the cause. If this approach surrendered some of the moral high ground women had been able to stake out, it may have ensured the victories of these years.[8]

After passage of the Nineteenth Amendment, women began to participate in political parties, but they often found their most important allies outside of mainstream politics. Women's political "friends" were likely to be fellow reformers or those who took an even more radical perspective. The Socialist Party, for example, supported women's suffrage, as did other groups involved in the Progressive movement. The question of whether to ally with mainstream political forces led to theoretical, strategic, and tactical debates within the women's movement, which in some instances led to serious divisions. Moreover, the winner-take-all and single-member district aspects of the electoral system discouraged women from creating their own political party. Known as Duverger's law, a plurality (winner-take-all) electoral system coupled with a single-member district system conspires to create two political parties rather than three or even more. Third parties have little chance of capturing the only seat in a single-member district, and thus voters who might otherwise vote for a third party switch to voting for one of the two majors parties so as not to "waste" their vote.[9]

Women's political activity in the 1920s and 1930s was thus limited to lobbying political parties at the local level and participating in reform movements; women also held meetings and attended trials. But many of the hoped-for gains in access to educational opportunity and to economic and political power never really materialized. Instead, women often wound up in a separate sphere of women's bureaus, auxiliaries, and occupations. As Matthews puts it, "women who thought they were establishing a beachhead in male-dominated institutions most often found themselves in some form of female ghetto."[10] This form of segregation plagued women until the beginnings of the modern feminist movement in the 1960s and the attendant changes in the lives of women—part of the cultural change discussed in Chapter 2. Women continued to participate in civic organizations, but they became more involved in partisan political activity (though still performing the menial tasks in political campaigns) and in the effort to influence public policies.

In the 1970s partisan politics was a "man's game," and civic movements were regarded as apart from politics. Since the 1970s, however, the gender gap in partisan political activity has been narrowing. Women's perceptions of the value of such activity have been influenced by public policies such as Title IX of the Education Act of 1972 (which prohibits discrimination on the basis of sex in admissions to all graduate and professional schools that receive federal funding), the battle for passage of the Equal Rights Amendment, the increase in women's employment outside the home, debate over abortion, the rise of groups such as the National Women's Political Caucus, and the opinions of women role models. But why do some women choose to participate and others do not? How are women who participate different from those who do not? Did they enjoy different opportunities? The next section addresses these questions.

Types of Political Women—the 1970s Onward

In the late 1970s Rita Mae Kelly and Mary Boutilier described three categories of political women: the private woman, the public woman, and the achieving woman. These ideal types were based on three dimensions related to socialization. The first dimension was the difference in sex-role concept between the traditional, passive woman and the modern, activist woman. The second dimension was the woman's control over her daily life. The third dimension was political saliency—that is, the extent to which politics and political activity were relevant to the woman's life.[11] Kelly and Boutilier argued that the most important prerequisite for the development of political behavior by women was a moderately activist (modern) sex-role concept. A woman who adhered to the traditional, passive sex-role concept, which prevented her from having much control over her daily life, was identified as the private woman. Acceptance of the passive role prevented her from behaving in nontraditional ways and encouraged her to participate only at the minimum level of civic obligation, such as voting. This type of woman tended to see politics as reflecting the cultural norms of a male-dominated socioeconomic and political structure. Kelly and Boutilier explained that politics was of little importance to this woman's life because it had little impact on her primary area of concern—the family. As a result, she was unlikely to do anything more than vote. The second type, the public woman, generally had a moderately activist sex-role concept, so she exhibited many types of political behavior depending on the amount of control she had over her daily life and the saliency of her political experiences. She saw political participation as more than just civic obligation. The public woman was likely to engage in partisan and nonpartisan volunteer activities such as organizing registration drives and participating in political campaigns. Her participation was often part-time and took a back seat to her responsibilities as a wife and mother; her husband's career, his attitudes, and his connections constrained her activities. The third type, the achieving woman, attained fame in the political sphere either by election to public office or by being part of a revolutionary group that opposed the existing political regime. She had a strong sense of personal political effectiveness, a high degree of control over her life space, and a strongly activist sex-role concept. The achieving woman ignored cultural norms about the traditional role of women in society, became a political actor, and used political channels to achieve social and political change. The achieving woman became a member of the political elite.

In sum, women who participated more actively in politics had three things in common: an attitude that did not accept the traditional view of a woman's proper role in society, opportunities for political participation, and a sense that political activity was something more than civic duty. Women who became members of the political elite changed the nature of political participation, not only for themselves but for all women.

Women's political participation has transformed since 1978, when Kelly and Boutilier created their categories of political women. Indeed, in the presidential election of 1996, which has been called the "Year of the Soccer Mom," women constituted one of the key electoral swing constituencies. A particular type of woman—concerned about family finances, the well-being of her parents, and the future of her children—was viewed as the key to victory. Since the late 1970s women have entered the work force in greater numbers to maintain or increase family income, have become increasingly involved in the care of aging parents, and have become aware that a whole range of external forces (television violence, street gangs, and crime) can harm their children. The "private woman" of Kelly and Boutilier now sees government as important to her family's well-being. Public policy issues such as tax cuts, the cost of higher education, access to abortion, women's health issues, and the future of Social Security are now part of her world. At the same time, there are now many women role models in a variety of fields—television reporters and news anchors, legislators, and Supreme Court justices. As educational, economic, and political opportunities increase, the culture becomes more accepting of women in these roles, and therefore the transition to "achieving woman" status becomes easier for each successive generation of women.

Breaking Down the Barriers to Political Participation

When a large group of people is excluded from policy making, as women were in the past, society loses the opportunity to take advantage of that group's intelligence, skills, talents, and perspectives. Yet despite all the compelling arguments in favor of increasing the participation of women in politics, women are still underrepresented among the political elite.

The percentage of women in statewide elective offices and state legislatures has at least doubled since 1979, and the percentage of women in the U.S. Congress has quadrupled (Table 6-1). However, women are still underrepresented given that they constitute more than half the population. In particular, the percentage of women in statewide office and the U.S. Congress seems to have plateaued since the elections of 1992 (The Year of the Woman) and 1996 (The Year of the Soccer Mom). What about these two elections spurred women's participation? Were the issues more relevant? Did Bill Clinton's calls for a more diverse government and the increasing influence of women's groups such as EMILY's List and the National Organization for Women have an effect? Perhaps the 1992 and 1996 elections tapped a reservoir of women interested in political office. And since then, has disillusionment set in?

The underrepresentation of women among the political elite appears to stem from two interrelated sets of problems—one that is environmental and structural and one that is attitudinal. Environmental and structural barriers include society's expectations that women have certain familial responsibilities, women's limited career opportunities, and the American electoral and party systems. Attitudinal barriers include attitudes of the general public concerning women's political participation, attitudes of the "political gatekeepers" (party leaders) who largely control the political process, and attitudes of women themselves toward political participation. The two sets of problems are interactive. The environmental and structural barriers erected in the path of women who would be political actors have in the past hindered the development of attitudes favorable to women's elite participation. The absence of women from the traditional political elite and the consequent lack of women role models (aside from those who were active in the turn-of-the-century social movements, which were not considered political) meant that the general public did not view women as possessing the qualities necessary to be political leaders, and those who controlled access to the party machinery and party nominations had trouble adapting to the thought of having women in the political elite.[12]

Robert Darcy, Susan Welch, and Janet Clark have described what they call the "eligibility pool"—an intangible group of potential political candidates judged on the basis of their education, occupation, personal contacts, and political ties.[13] Historically women have had difficulty gaining admission to this group because they were shut out of the educational institutions that would offer them the appropriate majors or programs; thus

TABLE 6-1

Women in Elective Office, 1979–2004 (percent)

Year	U.S. Congress	Statewide elective	State legislatures
1979	3.0	11.0	10.0
1981	4.0	11.0	12.0
1983	4.0	11.0	13.0
1985	5.0	14.0	15.0
1987	5.0	14.0	16.0
1989	5.0	14.0	17.0
1991	6.0	18.0	18.0
1993	10.0	22.0	21.0
1995	10.0	26.0	21.0
1997	11.0	26.0	22.0
1999	12.0	28.0	22.0
2001	14.0	27.0	22.0
2003	13.6	26.0	22.4
2004	13.6	26.0	22.4

Source: Center for American Women and Politics, *Women in Elective Office 2004,* fact sheet (Rutgers, N.J., 2004).

they could not prepare for careers in which they would develop personal and political contacts. Many women did not view political participation as desirable or did not consider themselves capable of elite participation. Some were inhibited from entering the political race and did not even seek their party's nomination in the primaries. Many women believed that running for and serving in an elective office were not appropriate roles for a woman. They had to deal with their own concern about the public's perception that they would be "abandoning their families"; consequently, many women entered political life only after their children had grown.[14] While women stayed at home and cared for children, men were developing contacts and gaining political know-how. Moreover, traditional women's occupations such as teacher and nurse did not introduce women to politically active individuals. By contrast, men were likely to pursue careers in business or law, which are generally considered to be training grounds for political candidates. The exclusion of women from decision-making and party leadership positions by the male-dominated political organizations meant that they were further denied the political skills and contacts necessary to be strong candidates. Women assumed the deck was stacked against them and were unlikely to seek public office.

Some studies have suggested that the major parties have been reluctant to nominate women candidates.[15] Nancy McGlen and Karen O'Connor have argued that there appeared to be a "hidden quota" as to the number of women that both the politicians and the public were willing to accept, and most often they were not executive positions. In addition, some government positions were designated as "women's positions" (in much the same way that some state political parties used to balance party tickets ethnically).[16] But should responsibility for these discriminatory attitudes lie with party leaders or with the public? Did party leaders believe that women were incapable of leading and making decisions? Or did they discourage women's candidacies because they feared that the voting public would reject women candidates as being incapable? Since a primary goal of the political party is to get its candidates elected to office, and because candidates have become increasingly dependent upon organizational campaign support (including financial contributions), party officials were reluctant to nominate women for fear that they would not be able to gain the support necessary to win. Women candidates thus found themselves in an unfortunate position: unable to attract large organizational contributions because organizations did not think women could win, women lost because they could not run a modern political campaign. Some women have inherited public positions on the death of their spouse, but they have usually been viewed only as caretakers who would finish out the spouse's term, although a few did win subsequent elections in their own right. Women are now committing themselves to political elite activity earlier (that is, not waiting until their children have grown) and are developing politically relevant careers and skills. Women's groups are now practicing "pipeline politics," helping women win lower-level positions that might translate into higher-level ones. (Senator Barbara Mikulski of Maryland, who worked her way up from a position in the Baltimore city government, identified herself after her 1986 victory as a "twenty-year overnight success story."[17])

The success of women in the elections of 1992 suggested that attitudinal barriers were beginning to fall. But the results of the off-year elections of 1994 (called "The Year of the Angry White Male") raised a significant question about whether women's earlier successes were an aberration or a harbinger. The results of the 1996 elections sent a mixed message for women. Record numbers of women ran for elective office, but percentage increases in the number of women in elective office were small. Since 1996 the increase in the number of women candidates has been small. For example, the number of women running for Congress in 1998 was two more

(131–10 Senate, 121 House candidates) than it was in 1996 (129–9 Senate, 120 House). The numbers were not significantly better for 2000 (128–6 Senate, 122 House) and 2002 (135–11 Senate, 124 House). The numbers were equally disappointing at the state level, where the number of women gubernatorial candidates in 1998 and 2002 was the same (10), the number of women candidates for lieutenant governor declined (from 25 to 21), the number of women candidates for secretary of state declined (from 24 to 13), and the number of women candidates for state treasurer remained the same (12). Only for state auditor (8 to 12) and state legislator (2,280 to 2,350) did the number of women candidates increase.[18]

A February 2004 Center for American Women and Politics (CAWP) fact sheet entitled "Summary of Potential Women Candidates 2004" estimated that 23 women could be candidates for the Senate in the 2004 election. Nine had filed (5 Democrats and 4 Republicans) and 14 were considering running (9 Democrats and 5 Republicans). In the House, 153 women were identified as potential candidates. Seventy-nine had filed (50 Democrats and 29 Republicans) and 74 were thought to be considering running (40 Democrats and 34 Republicans). At the state level 4 women were identified as considering running for governor (3 Democrats and 1 Republican), one woman (a Democrat) had filed and 5 women were identified as potential candidates for lieutenant governor (4 Democrats and 1 Republican), and it was estimated that 23 additional women would run for other statewide elective offices (12 Democrats, 10 Republicans, and 1 independent).[19] If many of the women identified as considering running do run, the number of women seeking elective office may increase, and concerns about reaching a plateau may fade. Explanations for why rates have plateaued include term limits, dissatisfaction with politics in general, and economic circumstances that prohibit women from moving into politics. Whatever the reason, the potential effect for women will be serious. In an October 2003 press release Debbie Walsh, director of CAWP, said, "Unless more women step up and run—whether in term-limited or non-term-limited states—the important gains we've made will be reversed."[20]

For many women, making the leap from observer to participant in the political process has been facilitated by women's organizations and women officeholders. Women's organizations, which include feminist organizations such as the National Organization for Women, the National Women's Political Caucus, and the Women's Campaign Fund, encourage women to seek political office and provide valuable campaign support, including financial assistance. Women involved in such organizations benefit from the opportunity to develop leadership skills. Susan J. Carroll and Wendy S. Strimling studied the attitudes of women who held elective positions at various levels of government. These women reported that they had found women's organizations (in particular, the National Women's Political Caucus, the National Organization for Women, and the League of Women Voters) to be especially important in encouraging them to seek public office. Approximately half of the women legislators and a quarter of the county commissioners surveyed belonged to feminist organizations, and about half of the women legislators either were or had been members of the League of Women Voters. As previously mentioned, women receive little support (financial or otherwise) from other political organizations, so the support of women's groups is particularly important, Carroll and Strimling suggest, for women who want to become active in party organizations.[21]

As both supporters and mentors, women officeholders have drawn increasing numbers of women into political activity. Carroll and Strimling point out that many women in elective office said they gained valuable political experience and skills at the side of other women officeholders— serving either as their legislative or administrative aides or as aides on their campaign staff. To the extent that women who got their political start in this manner provide the same assistance to other women, they establish an alternative entry point to politics, outside traditionally male-dominated organizations, and thus help to increase the number of women in politics.

Incumbency has in the past limited the opportunity of women (and men) to compete for positions that they would otherwise have a realistic chance of winning. Although the increase in negative public attitudes toward government and politicians and the calls for "change" in the system have made this less of a problem, incumbency is still a barrier for women because of their traditional lack of access to party nominations. Incumbents have always had extraordinary advantages such as name recognition, party support, and generous campaign funding that few challengers could overcome. Incumbents are especially difficult to dislodge in the many congressional districts that are relatively noncompetitive. Senators and representatives who have seniority also have increased institutional power that can be translated into benefits for their constituents, frequently resulting in increased interest group and popular support for those who show they can "deliver for the district." Some research has suggested that women have been about as successful in elections as men when party and incumbency of the opposing candidate are controlled for. [22]

Men vastly outnumber women in elite political positions partly because women have not run in as great numbers. Nearly two-thirds of the 1,000 likely voters polled by the National Women's Political Caucus said they think women have a tougher time winning elections than men. Caucus director Jody Newman, author of the study, suggests that this perception may contribute to women's reluctance to run for office.[23] The perception will change, of course, if more women win elections.

Negative public attitudes toward government and politicians in general could either help or hurt women candidates. Anti-incumbent feelings benefited women in the 1992 and 1994 elections but do not appear to have had much impact in later elections. Eventually women incumbents may be perceived not as the "outsiders" described by Barbara Boxer but as part of the "insider establishment." However, female incumbents and challengers can argue that the perspective they bring to policy problems and the solutions they propose are different from those of male incumbents and thus have an outsider attraction. Women do not have to worry just yet about being called insiders—the percentage of women in the ranks of the political elite is still nowhere near the percentage of women in the general population or the percentage of women who vote. But just how many women are part of the political elite?

WOMEN AS OFFICEHOLDERS

Women are becoming more abundant and more visible in political office. Women are now state governors, mayors of big cities, and campaign managers of national candidates. The number of women referenced on the front pages of newspapers, the proportion of front-page photographs featuring women, and the number of women interviewed as news sources have all increased.[24] Women now view elite political positions as attainable and enjoy a broad range of opportunities to pursue a political career.

Although the number of women who participate in politics continues to increase, the percentage of women who hold state and national legislative, executive, and judicial positions is still relatively small. The increase in the number of women in judicial positions and in appointed administrative positions has largely been the result of women's increased access to legal education and professional opportunities. Women now have available to them a path to the political elite that was formerly reserved for men. As previously mentioned, women who attain elite positions can serve as mentors for the women members of their staffs and appoint women to positions of political power, thus further increasing opportunities for women.

Although appointments of women at the national level capture most of the public attention, gains for women have been greatest at the state and local levels. Local issues such as crime, the quality of education, environmental hazards, and cleaner streets are what initially spur many people to take political action. Many citizens feel that their ability to influence national issues is limited by such factors as access, time, connections, and money. This is generally not the case at the local level, for people are more likely to understand the dynamics of a local problem and to know where to go to fix it, as well as who the key players are in influencing a decision. In the not-too-distant past, local politics was, for many women, the only avenue to political participation. For many women today, it is still the most accessible. Moreover, the local level is where many of the problems that are of most concern to women are addressed, and consequently where many women are introduced to political combat.

In many respects, the community activities in which many women participate enable them to gain useful training for their political careers, because they often meet like-minded women activists who have experience in grassroots organizing. At the same time, these types of political participation may reinforce in women an approach to politics that is distinct from that of men, influencing not only the issues women pursue but the behaviors they exhibit (deemphasizing partisanship and emphasizing cooperation to achieve common objectives) once they are elected or appointed to government positions.

The remainder of this chapter focuses on women in the judicial system, women in the legislatures, and women in state and local government and the different avenues they have pursued in achieving success.

The Judicial System

It is in the judicial system (local, state, and national) that women have made their largest gains and where the impact of cultural change can be seen most clearly. At the national level, the most well-known success stories are those of Supreme Court Justices Sandra Day O'Connor and Ruth Bader Ginsburg and former Attorney General Janet Reno, who were appointed to their positions by both Democratic and Republican presidents. At the local and state levels, women have worked their way up to positions of power and authority in prosecutors' offices, in local courts, and in the state attorney's office.

Women's access to a legal education accounts for most of the increase in women officeholders in the judicial system. Title IX of the Education Act of 1972 threw open the doors of law school to women, and their enrollment increased tenfold.[25] But as Earlean McCarrick points out, "More than the passage of time and an increasing number of women lawyers are necessary for women to achieve positions of power in proportion to their numbers. . . . That will require greater receptivity to women on the part of the 'opportunity structure'—those who participate in selecting judges and in securing for young law students and lawyers those positions which put them in line for selection as judges."[26] Jimmy Carter was the first U.S. president to open up the judicial system to women. Although he did not have the opportunity during his one term to appoint the first woman to the Supreme Court, he substantially increased the number of women appointees to federal courts, district courts, and appeals courts. Relatively fewer women were appointed during the presidencies of Ronald Reagan and George Bush; however, Reagan was the first president to appoint a woman (Sandra Day O'Connor) to the Supreme Court. With the election of Bill Clinton in 1992 and his emphasis on having a government that reflects the diversity of society, women gained another seat on the Supreme Court (Ruth Bader Ginsburg), the cabinet position of attorney general (Janet Reno), and numerous judicial nominations. During the Clinton presidency, partisanship in the judicial nomination and confirmation process increased even though Clinton's nominees were generally considered to be less ideological than the nominees of either Ronald Reagan or George Bush. Ideological and partisan battles continue in the nomination and confirmation process, and ideology has become more important than gender diversity.

Some women in the judicial system have received favorable reviews from their peers and the general public. Marcia Clark, one of the lead prosecutors in the O. J. Simpson trial, was generally applauded for her legal skills (even though some observers appeared to be more interested in her hairstyle and her ability to balance her public and private lives). Some critics initially argued that Janet Reno's appointment was intended to meet a quota rather than to fill a position, but for the most part she drew praise for her decisiveness and her willingness to accept responsibility for her decisions in such actions as the Branch Davidian crisis in Waco, Texas; the "Travelgate" problems of the Clinton administration; and the controversial decision to return Elian Gonzalez to his father in Cuba. The judicial system is a key arena where issues of importance to women (such as spousal abuse, date rape, nonpayment of child support, and access to health care services) are decided on a regular basis, and thus one where women can be influential. McGlen and O'Connor have analyzed the impact of Sandra Day O'Connor's appointment to the Supreme Court. Although Republican president Ronald Reagan appointed her and most people consider her to be part of the Court's conservative bloc, Justice O'Connor has supported the positions of women's rights advocates in the majority of sexual discrimination cases decided by the Court. She also wrote the majority opinion reaffirming a woman's right to have an abortion when the decision in *Roe v. Wade* (1973) was challenged in *Planned Parenthood of Southeastern Pennsylvania v. Casey* (1992).[27]

Scholars who have explored the impact of women on the judicial system have returned mixed results. Most judicial scholars have found little evidence that women judges' voting behavior is similar to that of men; indeed male judges are often more supportive of women's rights issues than women are. Susan Gluck Mezey concludes "there is little evidence to support the claim that women judges 'act for' women. Rather, the scholarship indicates that gender has little effect on judicial voting, and it is unlikely that the appearance of more women on the bench will prod the federal courts into becoming more responsive to the voices of women in society."[28]

The Legislature

Although women still hold a relatively small percentage of the seats in Congress and the state legislatures, women have begun the transition from political oddity to legislative force. Figure 6-1 shows the increase in the number of women in Congress since 1967. The number of women senators increased twofold from 1989 to the present, while the House of Representatives saw a sevenfold increase. An impressive increase, but women are still woefully underrepresented in Congress. Women account for only 13.6 percent of all members of Congress. Of the 73 women serving in the 108th Congress, 18 (24.7 percent) are women of color (11 African American women and 7 Latinas) and all serve in the House of Representatives. Historically, 29 women of color have served in Congress (20 African Americans, 2 Asian American/Pacific Islanders, and 7 Latinas). One, Carol Moseley-Braun, D-Ill., was the first woman of color to serve in the Senate. She lost her reelection bid in 1998 but remains active politically. She was the only woman candidate from a major party running for president in 2004.

FIGURE 6-1
Number of Women in Congress (90th–108th Congresses)

Number of women

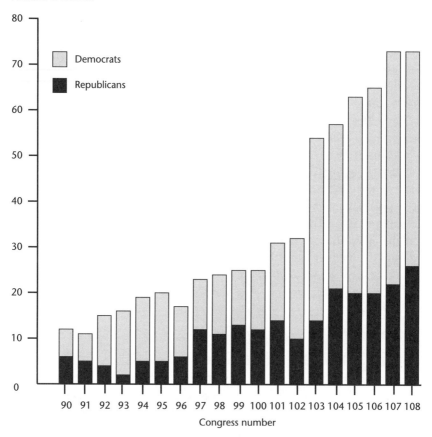

Source: Center for American Women and Politics, *Women in the U.S. Congress 2004,* fact sheet
(Rutgers, N.J., 2004).

Cultural change would argue that as the number of women in legislatures increases, their ability to become leaders should increase as well. Nancy Pelosi exemplifies this evolution. Pelosi, representative from the Eighth Congressional District in California, comes from a family that values public service. Both her father and brother have served as mayors of Baltimore, Maryland. Pelosi's political career started after her children enrolled in school. She started by volunteering for the Democratic Party and served as the state and northern chair of the California Democratic

Party. From 1967 to 1987 she was the Democratic National Committee representative from California, and then she was chairwoman of the 1984 Democratic National Convention Host Committee. In 1987, after her five children were grown, she ran for and was elected to Congress. Pelosi served as House Democratic whip for one year and was responsible for the party's legislative strategy in the House. In 2002 her colleagues overwhelmingly elected her Democratic Leader of the House of Representatives. She is the first woman in history to lead a major party in the U.S. Congress.[29]

Since 1969 there has also been a steady increase in the percentage of women in the state legislatures, as shown in Figure 6-2. Women hold 1,665 of the 7,382 (22.4 percent) state legislative seats. Women of color are 4.1 percent of all state legislators and are 304 or 18.4 percent of all women state legislators (86 senators and 218 representatives); all but seventeen are Democrats. The percentages of women in the state legislatures in 2004 are given in descending order in Table 6-2. In all but five states (South Carolina, Alabama, Kentucky, Mississippi, and Oklahoma), women hold a higher percentages of seats than they do in Congress. This is logical, as we would expect this sort of cultural change to begin locally. The expectation that women will increase their numbers in Congress is realistic given the increasing number of women entering politics at the local and state levels. As shown in Table 6-2, six of the ten states with the smallest percentages of women in the state legislature in 2004 are in the South, and six of the ten states with the highest percentages are in the West. Some research suggests that state legislatures with significant numbers of women operate differently than do those with small numbers of women, but the evidence is inconclusive.[30]

Legislatures have traditionally been the preserve of men and have operated largely as de facto men's social clubs. Bargaining, accommodation, and compromise grease the wheels of the legislative process in a pluralistic society, and these work best in an atmosphere of amiability and collegiality. Women in this social club environment are likely to feel like outsiders or strangers (as did Barbara Boxer). However, their perseverance is important, for how can a policymaking body that is not representative of the population produce policies that reflect a wide range of perspectives?

Since the 1970s, when women began to win legislative elections, some interesting research has shown changes in the sociodemographic characteristics of women legislators and the types of legislative positions (committee and leadership) they have attained. Irwin N. Gertzog has observed a drop in the number of women who succeed to the positions of their

FIGURE 6-2
Women in State Legislatures, 1971–2004

Women as a percentage
of state legislatures

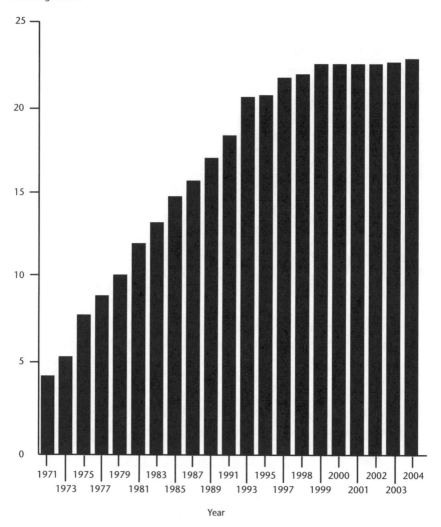

Year

Source: Center for American Women and Politics, *Women in State Legislatures 2004,* fact sheet (Rutgers, N.J., 2004).

TABLE 6-2
Women in State Legislatures, 2004 (percent)

State rank	State	Women	State rank	State	Women
1	Washington	36.7	26	Georgia	21.6
2	Colorado	34.0	27	Missouri	21.3
3	Maryland	33.5	28	Iowa	20.7
4	Vermont	31.1	29	North Carolina	20.6
5	California	30.0	30	Ohio	20.5
5	Oregon	30.0	31	Rhode Island	20.4
7	New Mexico	29.5	32	Alaska	20.0
8	Connecticut	29.4	33	Texas	19.3
9	Delaware	29.0	34	West Virginia	18.7
10	Nevada	28.6	35	Nebraska	18.4
11	Kansas	27.9	36	Indiana	18.0
12	Arizona	27.8	37	Wyoming	17.8
13	Illinois	27.7	38	Tennessee	17.4
14	Hawaii	27.6	39	Louisiana	16.7
15	Minnesota	27.4	40	North Dakota	16.3
15	New Hampshire	27.4	40	Arkansas	16.3
17	Wisconsin	27.3	42	South Dakota	16.2
18	Maine	26.9	43	New Jersey	15.8
19	Idaho	26.7	44	Virginia	14.3
20	Massachusetts	25.5	45	Pennsylvania	13.8
21	Florida	25.0	46	Oklahoma	12.8
22	Montana	24.7	47	Mississippi	12.6
23	Michigan	23.6	48	Kentucky	10.9
24	New York	22.2	49	Alabama	10.0
25	Utah	22.1	50	South Carolina	9.4

Source: Center for American Women and Politics, *Women in Elective Office 2004,* fact sheet (Rutgers, N.J., 2004).

deceased husbands, a jump in the number of married women, a drop in the number of women from political families or wealthy families, a jump in the number of women who are lawyers, and another jump in the number of women who have held prior elective positions.[31] In the 1920s a woman was considered only a temporary replacement for her deceased husband while the party decided which man would take over the seat in the next election; however, today she is likely to seek the office after a successful political career at other levels (state and local) or in other branches (executive and judicial). Gertzog identifies these women as "strategic politicians" and describes them as "experienced, highly motivated career public servants who carefully calculate the personal and political benefits of running for higher office, assess the probability of their winning, and determine the personal and political costs of defeat before deciding to risk the positions they hold to secure a more valued office." [32] Women who attain congressional positions are thus influenced by the changing political culture and the increasing opportunities available to them.

Gertzog analyzes the gender role orientations (gentlewoman, neutral, and feminist) and legislative role orientations (amateur, professional, and colleague) of women in Congress and develops three basic role orientations: the gentlewoman amateur, the neutral professional, and the feminist colleague. A woman member of Congress may fit any of these three categories at any time, but there is generally a historical pattern that is related to the number of women in the legislature. The gentlewoman amateur tends to be a traditional woman who accepts the subordinate gender role and has little interest in legislative activity or legislative experience. This category best describes the women of the 1960s and 1970s who, at most, performed some of the constituency service tasks associated with the legislative process.

The neutral professional role generally refers to women who entered Congress when the number of women in Congress was still small. Many were career politicians who had succeeded in an unfriendly political culture; they were hesitant to pursue issues or agendas that would be identified as specific to women, so they tried to maintain a low profile. They knew that they were being held to a different standard than were men and would be subjected to extraordinary scrutiny. This role thus combines an inhibited gender role with a cautionary legislative role. Gertzog suggests that neutral professionals knew that "as members of a small, conspicuous minority, they would be operating within a goldfish bowl. Behavior that would be overlooked or quickly forgotten if engaged in by a male representative would trigger derision or worse if enacted by a congresswoman. There were simply too many House members and constituents who did not need much of an excuse to interpret their activities according to a female stereotype." [33] Many of these women devoted a large chunk of their time to constituency service and hoped eventually to benefit from the seniority system, which then worked to the advantage of their male colleagues. Such behavior was only a slight improvement over that of the gentlewoman amateur. According to Gertzog, neutral professionals were still opting "for the subordinate status that females have traditionally held in their relationships with males. For underlying these efforts carefully to manage their behavior and avoid calling attention to their gender was the more fundamental objective of not upsetting men. They wanted to be effective legislators, and they could not gain that reputation by 'rocking the boat.' " [34] The neutral professional was thus a victim of an institution dominated by men.

The feminist colleague role, which began to emerge during the 1970s, combines a feminist gender role with an activist legislative role. The feminist perspective of these legislators influences their legislative behavior and their analysis of public policy. They do not defer to their male colleagues and have created an organization within Congress to support women's issues (the Congressional Caucus for Women's Issues). As a result of their efforts, Congress now addresses social issues such as spousal and child abuse and sexual harassment, which have historically been outside the domain of national policy. Gertzog describes the impact that feminist colleagues have had on congressmen: "Male members' understanding of their representative responsibilities has . . . been undergoing change. Congressmen have become less likely to ignore or treat cursorily the women's constituency, and they are much less diffident today about identifying with and even dramatizing their support for feminist causes." [35]

The successes of women in the legislative arena have implications for the individual women who aspire to political office, for women as a group, and for society as a whole. Sue Thomas predicts that

> As the proportion of women in governing bodies increases, the progress women have already made toward individual and group goals will be nearly complete. Female representatives effectively meet the needs of their constituents through service and legislative action, contribute significantly and meaningfully to policy debates, earn respect from their colleagues, and master the legislative process. As their numbers increase further, individual goals related to higher ambition will accelerate and legislative leadership will, more often, become the realm of women. [36]

Women's relatively recent success in capturing legislative seats is probably the greatest indication of the changing political culture. The experience of Barbara Boxer and her colleagues will likely never have to be repeated.

State and Local Governments

According to the Center for American Women and Politics, women held 81 (or 25.7 percent) of the 315 available statewide elective executive offices in 2004. This category does not include state-level appointed positions such as those in the cabinet, on boards of trustees, or in the judicial branch; nor does it include elective positions in the judiciary, on university boards of trustees, and on state boards of education. Overall, forty-eight of the fifty states have had women elected to statewide executive office (Maine and West Virginia are the exceptions). Among the 81 positions (36 Democrats, 42 Republicans, 3 independent) are 8 governors (5 Democrats, 3 Republicans), 17 lieutenant governors (7 Democrats, 10 Republicans), 5 attorneys general (4 Democrats, 1 Republicans), 10 secretaries of state (6 Democrats, 4 Republicans), 9 state treasurers (3 Democrats, 6 Republicans), 8 state auditors (3 Democrats, 5 Republicans), 3 state comptrollers (1 Democrats, 2 Republicans), 9 chief state education officers (4 Democrats, 2 Republicans, 3 nonpartisan), and 12 other types of state commissioner (3 Democrats, 9 Republicans).[37]

The preeminent elective executive position in every state is that of governor. As chief executive of the state, the governor generally has a wide range of powers and responsibilities, including appointive and veto powers and budget authority; the governor plays a role in the legislative process as well. In some states, the governor is the only official (with the exception of the two senators) elected statewide, and even when the governor is one of a number of statewide elected officials, he or she is generally the focus of media attention in the state. In the late 1800s many thought of governors as "good-time Charlies." But as Larry Sabato points out, "Once the darlings of the society pages, governors today are more concerned about the substantive work of the office than about its ceremonial aspects. . . . Once ill-prepared to govern and less prepared to lead, governors have welcomed into their ranks a new breed of vigorous, incisive, and thoroughly trained leaders."[38] Some would argue that the governorship used to be the pinnacle of the "good old boys" political network in most states. The man who attained this position had made many friends among party bosses and party activists, had name recognition as a result of media attention, and had access to money—all of which enabled him to successfully compete for the office. Virtually all these advantages would have been denied to women. Since the 1970s, however, women have been increasingly successful in gubernatorial races. Some of this success can be traced to changes in the nature of the governorship as described by Sabato and to the changing opportunities for women.

Altogether twenty-six women (seventeen Democrats, nine Republicans) have served as governors in twenty-one different states. Three replaced their husbands, six became governor through constitutional succession, and seventeen were elected to the office in their own right. The first woman to be elected governor was Nellie Taylor Ross, a Democrat from Wyoming (the first state to enfranchise women). She was elected to serve the two years that remained of her deceased husband's term and was defeated in the next election (1926). Miriam "Ma" Ferguson (D-Texas, 1925–1927) and Lurleen Wallace (D-Ala., 1966–1968) were elected as surrogates for their husbands, who could not run for reelection. The route to the governorship for these women reflected the political culture of their times. Women were not seen as viable candidates in their own right but as substitutes or stand-ins for their husbands. The fact that Ross and Ferguson became governors in the 1920s was remarkable.

The eight women governors serving in 2004 are literally and metaphorically all over the map, evidencing the depth of women's recent success in statewide elective office. Kathleen Blanco (Democrat), who won the governorship of Louisiana in 2003, also served in the state legislature (eight years), as public service commissioner (two years), and as lieutenant governor (eight years). Jennifer Granholm (Democrat) won the Michigan gubernatorial race in 2002 after serving for four years as attorney general. Linda Lingle (Republican) won the Hawaii gubernatorial race in 2002. She ran unsuccessfully in 1998 after having served eight years as mayor of Maui County. Judy Martz (Republican) became governor of Montana in 2000 after serving four years as lieutenant governor of the state. Ruth Ann Miller (Democrat) won the gubernatorial race in Delaware in 2000. Previously she had served in the Delaware House of Representatives for eight years, in the Delaware Senate for ten years, and as lieutenant governor for eight years. Janet Napolitano (Democrat) captured the governorship of Arizona in 2002 after serving as attorney general for four years. Kathleen Siebelius (Democrat) won the 2002 Kansas gubernatorial race. She had served eight years in the Kansas House of Representatives and was elected Kansas insurance commissioner in 1994. Olene S. Walker (Republican) became Utah's first woman governor in 2003 after her predecessor stepped down to take a position in Washington, D.C. She was first elected lieutenant governor in 1992 and before that had served eight years in the Utah House of Representatives, where she also served as both assistant majority whip and majority whip. The range of elective experiences that these women had prior to becoming governor of their states demonstrates the variety of paths available to women. The position of lieutenant governor can be a stepping stone to the governorship, for it increases statewide exposure. In

2004 seventeen women hold the position of lieutenant governor. How many of these will become governor?

The appointment of a woman to an administrative position can have three important consequences: First, there is the potential for a multiplier effect; women appointed to these positions are free to appoint other women to line and staff positions in administrative agencies and statewide commissions. Second, such appointments increase the likelihood that women's issues and concerns will receive higher priority on the agendas of public agencies and commissions. Third, a gradual change in the culture becomes possible, beginning in the public organizations to which women are appointed. Longer-term effects include changes in women's attitudes toward careers in public service and changes in the public's attitude toward women in government.

Take Ann Richards, governor of Texas from 1991 to 1995. Joanne Rajoppi argues that Richards radically changed the culture of Texas state government. Her initial cabinet-level appointments and appointments to state commissions, drawn largely from her contacts within county government and the women's movement, were intended to fulfill her campaign promise that Texas state government would no longer be the preserve of white men. The appointees' diversity (20 percent Hispanic, 15 percent black, 46 percent female, plus several Asian and gay appointees) led Alison Cook to point out that "there is no denying that Richards' picks reflect the state's diverse population—a radical notion in Texas and one that may prove to be her most enduring legacy. Richards' appointments have also set a populist tone foreign to recent Texas politics, and agencies long cozy with the industries they police have begun to tilt citizenward."[39]

CONCLUSION

Dramatic changes have occurred in American political culture since 1920, when women gained the right to vote. Changes in gender role orientation and political attitudes, the increasing opportunities for women to participate in politics, and an attitudinal and an occupational climate more supportive of women's equality have altered the gender ratio of the institutions of political power. Although women are still not represented in proportion to their numbers, they have made enormous inroads into previously all-male domains. In the judicial and legal systems, in legislatures, and in state and local governments, women have begun to occupy positions in numbers significant enough to enable them to influence the cultures of these institutions, the ways they operate, and the policies they produce.

The increasing numbers of women in the political elite, although a relatively recent phenomenon, is also a significant one. Many scholars still question what its long-term effects will be,[40] but it is obvious that the views of mayor Landrieu in the opening of this chapter do not reflect today's political culture. The increased educational, economic, and political opportunities that have become available to women since the 1960s have changed women's perceptions of their abilities to win public office, as well as the public's perception of women's political viability and political acumen. After the successes of women candidates in the elections of 1992, many felt that a watershed had occurred and that women's future in politics appeared to be secure. But the outcome of the 1994 off-year elections and the criticisms leveled against some women political actors (for example, their characterization as "feminazis" by conservative talk show host Rush Limbaugh) have raised some serious questions about the future of women's role in politics. The next chapter discusses the potential roadblocks to women's continued successes.

SUGGESTIONS FOR FURTHER READING

In Print

Boxer, Barbara, with Nicole Boxer. 1994. *Strangers in the Senate: Politics and the New Revolution of Women in America.* Washington, D.C.: National Press Books.

Carroll, Susan J. 1994. *Women as Candidates in American Politics.* 2d ed. Bloomington: Indiana University Press.

Cohen, Cathy J., Kathleen B. Jones, and Joan C. Tronto. 1997. *Women Transforming U.S. Politics: Sites of Power/Resistance.* New York: New York University Press.

Darcy, Robert, Susan Welch, and Janet Clark. 1994. *Women, Elections, and Representation.* 2d ed. Lincoln: University of Nebraska Press.

Gertzog, Irwin N. 1995. *Congressional Women: Their Recruitment, Integration, and Behavior.* 2d ed. Westport, Conn.: Greenwood Press.

Mandel, Ruth B. 1981. *In the Running: The New Woman Candidate.* New York: Ticknor and Fields.

Matthews, Glenna. 1992. *The Rise of Public Woman: Woman's Power and Woman's Place in the United States, 1630–1970.* New York: Oxford University Press.

Phillips, Anne. 1991. *Engendering Democracy.* University Park: Pennsylvania State University Press.

Rajoppi, Joanne. 1993. *Women in Office: Getting There and Staying There.* Westport, Conn.: Bergin and Garvey.

Ross, Karen, ed. 2002. *Women, Politics, and Change.* New York: Oxford University Press.

Thomas, Sue. 1994. *How Women Legislate.* New York: Oxford University Press.

Tolchin, Susan, and Martin Tolchin. 1974. *Clout: Womanpower and Politics.* New York: Coward, McCann, and Geoghegan.

Tolleson-Rinehart, Sue, and Jyl J. Josephson, eds. 2000. *Gender and American Politics: Women, Men, and the Political Process.* Armonk, N.Y.: M. E. Sharpe.

Witt, Linda, Karen M. Paget, and Glenna Matthews. 1994. *Running as a Woman: Gender and Power in American Politics.* New York: Free Press.

On the Web

Center for American Women and Politics. *www.rci.rutgers.edu/~cawp.* The center is a unit of the Eagleton Institute of Politics at Rutgers, The State University of New Jersey. This Web site provides access to a vast array of information about the status and prospects of women in government and politics at all levels.

EMILY's List. *www.emilyslist.org.* Founded in 1985, EMILY's List (Early Money Is Like Yeast) List is the nation's largest grassroots political network, raising campaign contributions for Democratic women candidates who support abortion rights and helping mobilize women voters.

League of Women Voters. *www.lwv.org.* This site supports informed political participation and has information on current political issues.

National Organization for Women. *www.now.org.* The NOW Web site contains up-to-date material on women's issues and planned political actions.

National Women's Political Caucus. *www.nwpc.org.* The caucus recruits, trains, and supports pro-abortion-rights women candidates for elected and appointed offices at all levels of government regardless of party affiliation. It also provides campaign training for candidates and campaign managers as well as technical assistance and advice.

NOTES

1. Susan Tolchin and Martin Tolchin, *Clout: Womanpower and Politics* (New York: Coward, McCann, and Geoghegan, 1974), 13–30.

2. Barbara Boxer with Nicole Boxer, *Strangers in the Senate: Politics and the New Revolution of Women in America* (Washington, D.C.: National Press Books, 1994), 32, 35.

3. For an expanded discussion of these ideas, see Nel Noddings, "The Gender Issue," *Educational Leadership* 49, no. 4 (December 1991–January 1992): 65–70.

4. Richard Neustadt, *Presidential Power* (New York: Wiley, 1964), 33–57.

5. Camilla Stivers, *Gender Images in Public Administration: Legitimacy and the Administrative State* (Newbury Park, Calif.: Sage Publications, 1993), 59.

6. George Will, "The Politics of Manliness," *Washington Post,* January 29, 2004, A29.

7. Glenna Matthews, *The Rise of Public Woman: Woman's Power and Woman's Place in the United States, 1630–1970* (New York: Oxford University Press, 1992).

8. Ibid., 173.

9. For a discussion of Duverger's Law, see Alan Ware, *Political Parties and Party Systems* (New York: Oxford University Press, 1996), 190–193.

10. Matthews, *The Rise of Public Woman,* 177.

11. Rita Mae Kelly and Mary Boutilier, *The Making of Political Women* (Chicago: Nelson-Hall, 1978), 61–72. Although this study is based on earlier data, the three categories help to demonstrate the changes that have occurred in women's political participation.

12. Nancy E. McGlen and Karen O'Connor, *Women's Rights: The Struggle for Equality in the Nineteenth and Twentieth Centuries* (New York: Praeger, 1983), 115.

13. Robert Darcy, Susan Welch, and Janet Clark, *Women, Elections, and Representation,* 2d ed. (Lincoln: University of Nebraska Press, 1994), 105.

14. McGlen and O'Connor, *Women's Rights,* 118.

15. Ibid., 120.

16. Ibid., 121.

17. Susan M. Hartmann, *From Margin to Mainstream: American Women and Politics since 1960* (New York: Knopf, 1989), 171–173.

18. Data from Center for American Women and Politics, *Summary of Women Candidates for Selected Offices 1970–2002* (New Brunswick, N.J.: Eagleton Institute of Politics, Rutgers University, 2004), www.rci.rutgers.edu/~cawp/Facts/CanHistory/can_histsum.pdf.

19. Ibid.

20. Center for American Women and Politics, *To the Point: Fewer Women Running in State Elections than in Previous Years,* reports the Center for American Women and Politics at Rutgers, press release, October 27, 2003, www.rci.rutgers.edu/~cawp/News/CAWPpress10-03.html.

21. Susan J. Carroll and Wendy S. Strimling, *Women's Routes to Elective Office: A Comparison with Men's* (Rutgers, N.J.: Center for American Women and Politics, 1983), 83–109, 136–137. The League of Women Voters (whose membership includes both men and women) does not support or endorse candidates (of either gender). Women must resign as officers of the League of Women Voters if they become candidates for political office.

22. National Women's Political Caucus, "Perception and Reality: A Study Comparing the Success of Men and Women Candidates" (Washington, D.C.: National Women's Political Caucus, 1994).

23. Jody Newman, "Perception and Reality: A Study Comparing the Success of Men and Women Candidates, Executive Summary" (Washington, D.C.: National Women's Political Caucus, 1994).

24. Pippa Norris, "Through a Gendered Lens: Media Framing of International Women Leaders" (paper presented at the meeting of the American Political Science Association, San Francisco, August 1996.)

25. Earlean McCarrick, "Women and the Criminal Justice System," in M. Margaret Conway, David W. Ahern, and Gertrude A. Steuernagel, eds., *Women and Public Policy: A Revolution in Progress* (Washington, D.C.: CQ Press, 1995), 172.

26. Ibid., 173.

27. Nancy E. McGlen and Karen O'Connor, *Women, Politics, and American Society* (Englewood Cliffs, N.J.: Prentice-Hall, 1995), 93.

28. Susan Gluck Mezey, "Gender and the Federal Judiciary," in Sue Tolleson-Rinehart and Jyl J. Josephson, eds., *Gender and American Politics: Women, Men, and the Political Process* (Armonk, N.Y.: M. E. Sharpe, 2000), 223.

29. Information from Eighth Congressional District of California Web site of Rep. Nancy Pelosi, www.house.gov/pelosi/biography/bio.html, April 12, 2004.

30. For an excellent survey of the literature on this subject, see Sue Thomas, *How Women Legislate* (New York: Oxford University Press, 1994).

31. This discussion is drawn from Chapters 2 and 3 of Irwin N. Gertzog, *Congressional Women: Their Recruitment, Integration, and Behavior,* 2d ed. (Westport, Conn.: Greenwood Press, 1995).

32. Ibid., 4.

33. Ibid., 254.

34. Ibid., 256–257.

35. Ibid., 260.

36. Thomas, *How Women Legislate,* 155.

37. Center for American Women and Politics, *Statewide Elective Executive Women 1996* (New Brunswick, N.J.: Eagleton Institute of Politics, Rutgers University, 1996).

38. Larry Sabato, *Goodbye to Good-Time Charlie: The American Governor Transformed, 1950–1975* (Washington, D.C.: CQ Press, 1983), 2.

39. Joanne Rajoppi, *Women in Office: Getting There and Staying There* (Westport, Conn.: Bergin and Garvey, 1993), 94. Ann Richards was a casualty of the Republican landslide in the 1994 off-year elections.

40. See, for example, Thomas, *How Women Legislate,* 149–158.

CHAPTER 7

Women, Politics, and Cultural Change

Change is the key word to use in characterizing the differences in the lives of three generations of women—Eleanora Tomec, her daughters, and her granddaughters. It is also the key word to use in assessing the significance of change for women, culture, and political participation. There has been a gradual redefinition of what it means to be a woman. Some women still consider home and family to be the center of their lives. For others, career concerns dominate; but life may be a juggling act—sometimes joyful, sometimes depressing, always challenging—in which they attempt to meet the needs of family members, employers, and friends. Although more opportunities are now available, not all women have the same range of options; they still may be limited by class, age, and race. Many women have the motivation and the resources to participate in some form of political activity. Those who make a greater commitment may become active in their political party and even run for office, they may become members of the political elite, or they may participate in political protests.

In the centuries that separate Abigail Adams's entreaty to her husband to "remember the ladies" and Barbara Boxer's entreaty as one of the "strangers in the Senate," women have succeeded in opening the doors to political power. Those who have become part of the political elite are now "at the table" where issues of importance to women and to the nation—

health care, education, the environment, and foreign policy—are decided. But have increased political participation and access to positions of power and responsibility made a difference in women's lives? In the quality of life of most Americans? Have changes in society and in women's attitudes and beliefs revolutionized women's roles in the political arena? Has there been a change in the policy agenda or the political process? These are some of the questions this chapter addresses.

FROM THE PAST TO THE PRESENT

Elizabeth Cady Stanton, Eleanora Tomec, and Barbara Jordan led very different lives at different times in history. These women also differed in race, age, religion, education, employment, and marital status. Is it even possible to discuss commonalities, to view women's political participation as something that can have meaning beyond the lives of individual women? Gender both shapes and is shaped by culture, and it is commonalities of gender—what it means to be a woman who is influencing and influenced by American culture—that give legitimacy to this analysis.

In this book we have focused on fundamental cultural changes. Chapter 1 introduced the story of women's political participation in the United States. Although women were denied the right to vote until 1920, they had long participated in movements to bring about change. The Daughters of Liberty played a role in the American Revolution. Women were involved in the abolitionist movement before the Civil War and in other movements for social justice. Although women could not vote they were active politically, even when they had to work outside the mainstream or were confined to more "appropriate" roles for women.

The lives of Eleanora Tomec and her daughters illustrate some of the major cultural changes that have occurred in women's lives. Tomec was typical of her generation because she did not graduate from college. Her daughters, typical of their generations, did. Tomec's working life was somewhat atypical of her generation, but her profession was not. Her daughters' working lives, each different from the other, reveal the diversity of opportunities increasingly available to women—and the challenges they present. Politically, Tomec identified with party and faith, not gender. Although she was a regular voter, she participated in few political activities. Her daughters, both of whom identify less strongly with the Democratic Party and the Catholic Church than did their mother, vote regularly and have participated in peaceful demonstrations and other forms of political activity. They are more conscious of the role gender has played in their lives; the older daughter has reentered the work force after her divorce, the younger daughter holds a nontraditional job and delayed childbearing and marriage. The choices Tomec made about her life were based primarily on her roles as wife and mother. But her younger daughter did not delay or abandon her career plans to be a wife and mother. Instead, she had to navigate the unfamiliar waters of role change, trying somehow to be at once wife, mother, and employee.

In many respects, Tomec's daughters had more of the autonomy and self-determination that are the foundation of a liberal culture. But they had this advantage in large part because of their mother's contribution. Tomec recognized the value of an education, and it was her earnings from a secretarial job that financed her children's college educations and helped them launch their careers. Tomec's daughters were also able to take advantage of the opportunities that began to open up for women—opportunities not available to her.

Tomec's sacrifice has indirectly increased the opportunities of her granddaughters as well. Both of Tomec's granddaughters graduated from college and went on to graduate school. Each has traveled far more extensively than Tomec or her daughters. Tomec's personal decisions and political choices have had an impact, direct or indirect, on the lives of her daughters and granddaughters. They are also part of the larger impact women have had on American culture and politics. Political participation for Tomec meant primarily carrying out her civic duty by voting; for her daughters and granddaughters it means much more.

Cultural Change and Gender Consciousness

Cultural change influences how women acquire notions of gender-appropriate behavior, and these notions affect women's political participation (Chapter 2). Political socialization includes both direct and indirect political learning. The major agents of political socialization are family, school, and workplace, along with situational and structural factors. Gender and race can shape political beliefs and ambitions, as they did Barbara Jordan's. Three key concepts in the discussion of political socialization are acculturation, the social clock, and gender consciousness.

Acculturation, a term usually used to describe immigrants' adaptation to a new culture, is also used in the context of the historical foreignness of politics to women. Politics, which has traditionally been a male domain with a language dominated by metaphors of power, has been changed by the entry of women. The social clock refers to society's expectations for behavior that is appropriate at various stages of life. The lives of Barbara Jordan and of Eleanora Tomec and her daughters can be analyzed in this light. Women's political participation has been influenced by their gender consciousness—that is, how women define themselves as women.

Gender differences have been found in political attitudes and policy preferences (Chapter 3). Possible explanations for the existence of gender differences in political orientation include gender role socialization and the differential treatment of men and women on the basis of differences in educational attainment, occupation, and income. Data from public opinion surveys, such as the American National Election Studies, reveal some specific gender differences in public policy preferences on issues such as support for expansion or contraction of government programs and services, support for the use of force to solve problems, abortion policy, affirmative action, sexual harassment, and trustworthiness and effectiveness of the federal government. Men and women have also been found to differ in their knowledge about government and politics, their party identification, and their candidate preferences.

Women's group consciousness has been found to influence their political orientation and policy preferences (Chapter 4). Women have been categorized as feminists, potential feminists, and nonfeminists. Feminist orientation can affect political attitudes concerning a number of issues, such as abortion policy, sexual harassment, environmental programs, federally sponsored health care programs, and federal spending for child care and public education. Feminists tend to be more supportive than potential feminists or nonfeminists of these two spending programs, but there seems to be no significant difference among the three groups in support for foreign aid and federal funding for crime prevention and aid to the poor. These findings suggest the need to pay attention to differences in political orientation, both among women and between men and women.

Political Participation

Women's political participation can be analyzed in terms of their voting turnout and choices and involvement in political activities (Chapter 5). A number of trends emerge, reflecting the impact of employment and educational status on women's political participation. For example, women with different levels of education have different policy concerns. American National Election Studies data on presidential elections from 1952 to 2000 are the basis for a comparison of men's and women's participation in five types of political activities: working for a candidate or political party, contributing money, attending a political meeting or campaign rally, trying to persuade someone else to vote, and wearing a campaign button or displaying a campaign sticker. People sometimes participate in politics when asked to do so. Men are more likely than women to make campaign contributions. But men are also more likely than women to be asked to make such contributions. Women are more likely than men to vote, yet their rates of participation in other forms of political activity lag behind those of men. We must look beyond traditional forms of political participation, such as voting and campaigning, to find examples of women's political involvement. Women are frequently involved in community activities that, although not directly political, have political consequences. These activities enable them to acquire leadership skills that are useful in more traditional political activities. Theoretically, those who have the resources to participate are more likely to do so. The changes that have occurred in women's lives in education and employment are increasing women's resources, which may be linked to increasing political participation.

Women who develop feminist consciousness are more likely to become involved in some form of political activity. The evidence presented in Chapter 4 suggests that younger women, women who are better educated, and women who are employed are more likely to display feminist consciousness. Given women's increasing levels of education and participation in the work force, the possibility exists that feminist consciousness will also increase, and along with it, women's political participation.

As the political culture has changed, and as women's lives have changed, more women have become members of the political elite (Chapter 6). Although women continue to be severely underrepresented in proportion to their numbers in the general population, they are making progress in joining what previously has been a male domain. In the last three decades women have made dramatic strides in national and state legislatures and in statewide elective offices. Historically, women have had an impact on public policy even though they were denied entry into the political elite. Now that there are fewer attitudinal and structural barriers to membership, women will likely have a greater impact on public policy.

A male standard has dominated U.S. politics. Qualities traditionally associated with men, such as decisiveness and aggressiveness, have defined strong leadership. Qualities associated with women, such as compassion and compromise, have been linked with weak leadership. As the culture changes, and as more women enter the political elite, the popular notion of what it means to be a leader may also change. Cultural views of leadership may change with events. The terrorist attacks on September 11, 2001, may temporarily (or permanently) alter views of what it means to be a leader.

Many of the barriers to women's participation in the political elite are crumbling. The legal profession has traditionally been viewed as useful preparation for public office. As more women graduate from law school, more will be perceived as having the traditional qualifications for serving in the political elite. As more women run for and attain public office, women will increasingly be perceived as viable candidates and therefore attractive to potential donors. Political parties are also becoming more receptive to women candidates, and groups such as EMILY's List are helping women overcome financial barriers to running for office. (Money, ironically, has been referred to as the "mother's milk" of American politics.)

Women now hold elective or appointive positions at all levels and in all three branches of government. A society in which, little more than a century ago, more than half of the population was disenfranchised now has universal suffrage, and blacks and women are becoming part of the political elite. A revolution has taken place, but the question now is, how far have women yet to go?

THE OUTLOOK FOR WOMEN: POSITIVE SIGNS, NEGATIVE PORTENTS

To better understand the changes in gender roles that have occurred over the past few centuries and to assess women's progress, we should seek out the areas where women are making a difference and ascertain how they are doing so. Are they continuing to influence the outcome of elections, become a larger proportion of the political elite, and have an impact on public policy? What are the possible negative portents, such as opposition to some of the cultural changes that are taking place?

Women's Role in Elections

Since the beginning of the modern women's movement in the 1960s, women's political participation has burgeoned. The increase in voter turnout among women has created the potential for them to affect electoral outcomes. Since 1964 the number of women voters in presidential elections has exceeded the number of male voters; and beginning with 1980, the proportion of eligible women who voted in presidential elections has exceeded the proportion of eligible men. In the 2000 presidential election the number of women who reported voting exceeded the number of men who reported voting in every racial and ethnic group, including Asian/Pacific Islander, black, Hispanic, and white. Moreover, since 1986 a higher proportion of women than men have voted in nonpresidential election years.[1] Since the early 1980s a gender gap has existed in vote choice for candidates. If there is a significant gender gap in both turnout and vote choice, women may determine the outcome of an election.[2] In every presidential election since 1980, women have been more likely than men to support the Democratic candidate.[3]

Women played an important role in the elections of 1996, 2000, and 2002. In the 1996 presidential election, Clinton received 54 percent of the women's vote compared with Dole's 38 percent and independent candidate Ross Perot's 7 percent. As for men's votes, the difference between the two major candidates was minimal. Clinton received 43 percent, Dole received 44 percent, and Perot received 10 percent. Working women may have been the key to the presidential election. Indeed, in 1996 Ellen R. Malcolm, president of EMILY's List, observed that 1996 could be the year of the "angry woman voter": The "female counterpart of the 'angry white male'—the guy whose talk-radio-fueled anger dominated the 1994 election—is beginning to cause a commotion of her own. Alienated by the Republican 'revolution' on Capitol Hill and its attendant efforts to shred health, environmental, and social safety standards, she is hostile to the Republican Party [because of the stridency of the political discourse in Washington], but by no means a sure bet for Democrats."[4]

The 2000 elections also saw a gender gap, especially in the presidential race. Overall, 53 percent of men and 43 percent of women voted for George W. Bush, while 54 percent of women and 42 percent of men voted for Al Gore. Working women in particular preferred Gore over Bush by a margin of nineteen percentage points. Women voters also were responsible for the election of senators Hillary Clinton, D-N.Y.; Debbie Stabenow, D-Mich.; and Maria Cantwell, D-Wash. And there was also a gender gap in races for the House of Representatives where, overall, 53 percent of women compared to 44 percent of men voted for the Democratic congressional candidate in their district.[5]

Nonetheless, there is some evidence that women's support for Democratic candidates may be waning. In 2002 men continued to support Republicans, with 55 percent voting for Republican congressional candidates. Women's support for Republican candidates increased from 45 percent in 2000 to 50 percent in 2002, and the support for Republicans among married women was particularly strong at 56 percent compared to 39 percent of single women. According to the exit poll taken at the time of the elections, and it should be noted this poll had a number of problems, women supported Republican candidates because of their fear of terrorism and the downturn in the stock market. It is too early to determine if women's support for Republicans is a trend or was specific to this election.[6] There is some evidence to suggest that Republicans may be focusing on blue-collar men (the "Nascar Dad" strategy) and little evidence to suggest they are developing a strategy to appeal to women.[7]

Women's increased participation is evident in the funding of political campaigns. The number of political action committees (PACs) created to support women candidates increased from four in 1975–1976 to forty-eight in 1993 and fifty-five in 1996.[8] By 2003 there were forty-two PACs and donor networks that gave money primarily to women candidates or had a donor base composed primarily of women.[9] Women's PACs gave money to women candidates early in the campaign cycle, thus enabling them to organize a professional staff. This is surely one reason for the increased numbers of women winning elective office. After the 1996 elections, Malcolm announced: "We are thrilled that not one of our incumbent Democratic congresswomen lost. Our 45,000 EMILY's List members proved why Democratic women have become such a potent force in American politics by contributing $6.5 million to elect women candidates and $3 million to mobilize voters as part of our Women Vote! project."[10]

Another interesting development in the 2002 elections and also of potential significance in the 2004 elections concerned political donations by individual women. According to the Center for Responsive Politics, during the 2002 election cycle women with income separate from their spouses gave their money for the most part to Democrats, while women with no income of their own gave most of their donations to Republicans at about the same rate as male donors. Women with their own income gave 61 percent of their money to Democrats and 39 percent to Republicans, while women who listed no income of their own gave 55 percent to Republicans and 45 percent to Democrats.[11]

The number of successful women candidates has increased in electoral contests at all levels—local, state, and federal. The proportion of members of Congress who are women increased from 3 percent in 1979 to nearly 14 percent in 2003. Between 1979 and 2003, the proportion of women in statewide elective offices increased from 11 percent to 26 percent; and the proportion of women in state legislative offices during the same period increased from 10 percent to 22.3 percent. Almost 25 percent of the women serving in Congress are women of color, compared to 6.3 percent of women in statewide elective executive offices and 18.1 percent of female state legislators.[12]

Political Elites and Policy Making

On November 5, 2003, President Bush signed Public Law 108-105 (18USC1531), the Partial Birth Abortion Ban Act of 2003. At the signing ceremony, lawmakers influential in the bill's passage—all of whom were male—flanked the president on either side. The Associated Press photograph of the ceremony was widely disseminated in the print and electronic media. Did the president's advisers deliberately exclude women from the photo opportunity to reinforce an image of patriarchal dominance? Were there no female legislators in leadership positions guiding the bill's passage into law? Was it an oversight? These questions remain unanswered, but the photo highlights challenges still facing women today.

Still, the increased number of women in the political elite has probably led to an increased awareness among men in public office that women's issues demand their attention. Women in elective office have influenced both the policy agenda and policy outcomes. With regard to policy agenda, women legislators are more likely to emphasize issues that are important to women, such as health care, care of the elderly, housing, and education, and to support state and federal equal rights amendments. They tend to support abortion rights and the death penalty.[13] Both men and women in the legislatures recognize that women's efforts concerning these issues make a difference in legislative outcomes.[14] Women legislators may spend more time on, and allocate more staff to, constituency service activities.[15]

Men are more likely to name taxation and the budget as their most important legislative policy concerns. The degree to which women name women's issues as their top legislative priorities is related to ideology, occupation, age, and legislative seniority. (Such emphasis is more likely among liberals, women in traditionally female occupations, older women, and women who have served longer in the legislature.[16]) Women legislators from liberal districts are more supportive of women's issues than are men from liberal districts. However, women legislators from conservative districts are more supportive of such issues as health care and care for the elderly than are men from conservative districts. Democrats are more supportive of these issues than Republicans, but women legislators are more supportive than their male colleagues of the same party. Black women are more supportive of women's issues than are white women.[17]

Studies of state legislatures have found that women are more successful when they constitute more than a minimal percentage of a legislature's members—generally, at least 15–20 percent. The existence of a formal women's caucus in the legislature can also contribute to women's legislative success. Women can be more effective when they are appointed to leadership positions such as the head of a committee.[18] Women's legislative success is also a function of the number of campaign endorsements received from major women's groups and the number of legislators who are members of such groups.

With regard to policy outcomes, women members of Congress have enacted several policies that are relevant to women. Beginning in 1990 the Congressional Caucus for Women's Issues sought enactment of major policy changes in health care research, provision of health care services, and disease prevention programs because of the gender-based inequities that existed in such programs and in the funding allocated to medical research by the House and Senate Appropriations Committees.[19]

Female legislators have mastered legislative technique (as evidenced by their success in bill introduction and passage), proved their credibility by winning seats on the range of legislative committees and winning some leadership positions, achieved a reelection rate comparable to men's, increased their numbers, and succeeded in overcoming much of the overt discrimination against them. Although many benefits result from the direct efforts and successes of female legislators, arguably the most distinctive, dramatic, and fully developed contribution has been bringing issues that were heretofore considered marginal and of lesser significance squarely into the center of public agendas throughout the nation. The laws that address these issues have transformed the lives and options of many people, and without women in elective office, it is doubtful that these benefits would be available today. As women take their place as players on the political stage, society will likely become more tolerant of them in myriad positions of power: no longer will women in high-level, high-visibility positions be seen as exceptional. Young girls will grow up knowing that women can perform all of society's roles and that their sex will not limit their dreams. Increasing women's presence in the political sphere creates another benefit to public life generally: access to a greater diversity of ideas and experiences that fuel problem solving. Leaving any group out of policy formation and legitimization necessarily limits the range of ideas. It is hard to imagine a worse way to restrict the visions of a society.[20]

Women in public office exhibit a leadership style that encourages the inclusion of other perspectives. Women are also more likely to emphasize and attempt to increase citizen participation in policy making, particularly that of formerly excluded or underrepresented groups such as women and minorities.[21] Furthermore, women elected officials tend to make special efforts to hire women and to recruit them as candidates for public office.[22] Women governors and mayors tend to appoint more women to their staffs and to boards and commissions that are important in the creation, implementation, and enforcement of policy. A study of mayors (both men and women) in five large cities found that women tend to place greater emphasis on teamwork and collegiality.[23]

Until the 1980s few women were attorneys, and very few were judges. The increased enrollment of women in law schools as a consequence of the Higher Education Act Amendments of 1972 resulted in a gradual increase in the proportion of attorneys who are women and thus in the number of women appointed as judges at the municipal, state, and federal levels. President Jimmy Carter nominated forty women for federal judgeships—more women than were appointed by any prior president. However, by the end of his term in early 1981, only forty-six women were serving as federal judges. During President Ronald Reagan's eight years in office, he nominated only twenty-six women for federal judgeships, although there were 368 vacancies during that time. He did appoint the first woman—Sandra Day O'Connor—to the Supreme Court. President George Bush appointed fewer women to fill judicial vacancies than did President Reagan.[24] During President Bill Clinton's first year in office, more than 40 percent of his nominees for federal judicial appointments were women.[25] But by July 1995, only 16 percent of the federal judges were women.[26] As of the end of 2003, 80 percent of President George W. Bush's judicial nominees were men. Interestingly, women's groups have opposed some of the female nominees for their anti–women's rights positions.[27]

The research cited in Chapter 6, based on federal judges, suggests that a judge's gender has little impact on judicial voting. But research based on a wide range of judges, including federal and state judges and trial and appellate studies, suggests women judges are more likely than male judges to treat women lawyers in a nondiscriminatory manner and to decide in favor of women litigants in cases dealing with gender-related issues such as maternity leave, the rights of battered women, and sexual harassment at the place of employment.[28]

Since passage of the Nineteenth Amendment, women's role in the political process has changed dramatically. Especially since the mid-1960s, women's opportunities in education and employment have increased, and women have taken advantage of them. Although women do not yet have equal representation in all of the policymaking institutions, they no longer have to knock on the doors to political power. At all levels and in all three branches of government, women are making a difference.

NOTES

1. Center for American Women and Politics, *Sex Differences in Voter Turnout,* fact sheet (New Brunswick, N.J.: Eagleton Institute of Politics, Rutgers University, 2002).

2. In 1992 women's vote choices differed enough from those of men to elect Democrats Dianne Feinstein and Barbara Boxer in both of California's contests for the U.S. Senate. Sometimes, however, the gender gap is reversed, as in the 1992 senatorial race between Les AuCoin and Bob Packwood in Oregon; only 44 percent of women but 60 percent of men supported Packwood, who won the election. Center for American Women and Politics, *The Gender Gap,* fact sheet (New Brunswick, N.J.: Eagleton Institute of Politics, Rutgers University, 1994). Senator Packwood's resignation, effective October 1, 1995, followed a thirty-three-month inquiry by the Senate Ethics Committee into his alleged abuse of office, obstruction of justice, and sexual misconduct. *Congressional Quarterly Weekly Report* (January 6, 1996): 21.

3. Center for American Women and Politics, *The Gender Gap,* fact sheet (New Brunswick, N.J.: Eagleton Institute of Politics, Rutgers University, 1992). In 1992 men were significantly more likely than women to support third-party candidate Ross Perot. In the American National Election Study postelection survey, 16 percent of white women and 26 percent of white men reported voting for Perot. Only 3 percent of blacks reported voting for Perot. See Paul R. Abramson, John H. Aldrich, and David W. Rohde, *Change and Continuity in the 1992 Elections,* rev. ed. (Washington, D.C.: CQ Press, 1995), Table 5-1, 133.

4. Ellen R. Malcolm, "The 'Angry Woman Voter' May Change '96 Elections," *Philadelphia Inquirer,* March 8, 1996, www.emilyslist.org/talk/press3.htm.

5. Ibid.; Center for American Women and Politics, *Gender Gap in the 2000 Elections,* fact sheet (New Brunswick, N.J.: Eagleton Institute of Politics, Rutgers University, 2004).

6. Steve Saller, "Analysis: The Voting Gender Gap Narrows," *The Washington Times,* November 13, 2003, http://washingtontimes.com/upi-breaking/20031113-090231-4928r.htm.

7. See, for example, Arlie Hochschild, "Let Them Eat War," October 2, 2003, www.alternet.org/print.html?StoryID=16885.

8. Susan Roberts, "Women's PACs: Evolution, Operation, and Outlook" (paper prepared for the meeting of the Southern Political Science Association, Atlanta, November 1992). See also Center for American Women and Politics, *News and Notes* 9 (2): 18, and 10 (3): 6.

9. Center for American Women and Politics, *Women's PACs and Donor Networks: A Contact List,* fact sheet (New Brunswick, N.J.: Eagleton Institute of Politics, Rutgers University, 2003).

10. EMILY's List, "A Great Election Night for EMILY's List and Democratic Women," November 6, 1996, press release, www.emilyslist.org/news/press/110696.htm.

11. Center for Responsive Politics, "Gender Gap, GOP Edge in Small Donations Could Loom Big in 2004 Elections," June 27, 2003, press release.

12. Center for American Women and Politics, *Women in Elective Office 2003,* fact sheet (New Brunswick, N.J.: Eagleton Institute of Politics, Rutgers University, 2003). Center for American Women and Politics, *Women in Elective Office 2003,* fact sheet (New Brunswick, N.J.: Eagleton Institute of Politics, Rutgers University, 2003).

13. Sue Thomas and Susan Welch, "The Impact of Gender on Activities and Priorities of State Legislators," *Western Political Quarterly* 44 (June 1991): 445–457; Sue Thomas, "The Impact of Women on State Legislative Policies," *Journal of Politics* 53 (November 1991): 958–966; Debra L. Dodson and Susan J. Carroll, *Reshaping the Agenda: Women in State Legislatures* (New Brunswick, N.J.: Center for American Women and Politics, 1991), 5. See also Susan J. Carroll, ed., *The Impact of Women in Public Office* (Bloomington: Indiana University Press, 2001).

14. Dodson and Carroll, *Reshaping the Agenda,* 12.

15. Sue Thomas, "The Effects of Race and Gender on Constituency Service," *Western Political Quarterly* 44 (March 1992): 169–180.

16. Dodson and Carroll, *Reshaping the Agenda,* chap. 3.

17. Thomas, "Impact of Women"; Dodson and Carroll, *Reshaping the Agenda,* chap. 2.

18. Jeanie R. Stanley and Diane D. Blair, "Gender Differences in Legislative Effectiveness: The Impact of the Legislative Environment," in Debra L. Dodson,

ed., *Gender and Policymaking* (New Brunswick, N.J.: Center for American Women and Politics, 1991), 115–129.

19. Debra L. Dodson, Susan J. Carroll, Ruth B. Mandel, Katherine E. Kleeman, Ronnee Schreiber, and Debra Liebowitz, *Voices, Views, Votes: The Impact of Women in the 103rd Congress* (New Brunswick, N.J.: Center for American Women and Politics, 1995).

20. Sue Thomas, *How Women Legislate* (New York: Oxford University Press, 1994), 139–147.

21. Susan J. Carroll, Debra L. Dodson, and Ruth B. Mandel, *The Impact of Women in Public Office* (New Brunswick, N.J.: Center for American Women and Politics, 1991); Janet Boles, "Advancing the Women's Agenda within Local Legislatures: The Role of Female Elected Officials," in Dodson, *Gender and Policymaking,* 39–48.

22. Dodson and Carroll, *Reshaping the Agenda,* 3.

23. Sue Tolleson-Rinehart, "Do Women Leaders Make a Difference? Substance, Style, and Perceptions," in ibid., 93–102.

24. Nancy E. McGlen and Karen O'Connor, *Women, Politics, and American Society* (Englewood Cliffs, N.J.: Prentice-Hall, 1995), 91–92.

25. *American Bar Association Journal* (April 1994): 16.

26. H. T. Smith, "President's Page," *American Bar Association Journal* (July 1995): 8.

27. National Organization for Women, "NOW Opposes Extremist Judicial Nominees-Regardless of Gender," November 13, 2003, press release, www.now.org/press/11-03/11-13.html.

28. Elaine Martin, "Judicial Gender and Judicial Choices," in Dodson, *Gender and Policymaking,* 49–61.

Index

Abolition, 7, 9, 12, 113, 140
Abortion policy
  candidate positions on, 93
  educational attainment and, 45–46
  elective abortion, 45
  evangelical doctrine and, 40
  feminist orientation and, 76
  gender differences in opinion on, 41, 44–46,
    47
  government funding for, 45
  husband's permission, 45
  parental consent, 45, 76
  partial birth abortion, 76, 147
  political ideology and, 45–46
  political participation and, 114
  private women and, 116
  Supreme Court opinion, 2, 125
  traumatic abortion, 45
  women legislators and, 147
  women's opinions on, by feminist category,
    77–78
Abramson, Paul R., 62, 150
Acculturation, 29–30, 31, 141–142
Achieving women, 115–116
Adams, Abigail and John, 8, 87, 100, 113, 139
Affirmative action, 40, 41, 46, 48–50, 51
Afghanistan, 110
African Americans. See Blacks
Age
  age-appropriate behavior, 21
  gender consciousness and, 29
  marriage and, 1, 25
Agenda
  feminist, 39
  political, 30–31
Ahern, David W., 16, 17, 60, 61, 104, 138
AIDS research, 43
Albright, Madeleine K., 32
Aldrich, John H., 62, 150
Almond, Gabriel, 104
American National Election Studies, 44–45, 50,
  66–67, 75, 143
American Nurses Association, 95
American Revolution, 7, 140
American Woman Suffrage Association, 12

Andersen, Kristi, 33, 35
Anthony, Susan B., 11–12, 17, 113
Appointments, 122–123, 134, 149
Arrington, Theodore S., 104
Asian American/Pacific Islanders
  in Congress, 125
  education, 6
  income, 28
Atkeson, Lonna Rae, 34
Attitudes, political. See Political attitudes
Attitudinal barriers, 117, 119
AuCoin, Les, 150

Baby boomers, 29, 96
Baer, Judith A., 17, 61
Baker v. Carr (1962), 32
Baltimore, Lord, 8
Banks, Michael H., 34
Barnes, Samuel H., 104
Barnett, Irene, 33
Barriers to political participation, 24, 144
  attitudinal, 117, 119
  breaking down, 116–122
  environmental and structural, 117
Baxter, Sandra, 102
Beck, Paul Allen, 35
Beckwith, Karen, 102
Beliefs, 27, 40, 100
Bendyna, Mary E., 62, 103
Bennett, Linda L. M., 35
Bennett, Stephen E., 35
Birth rate, 1, 25
Blacks
  in Congress, 19–21, 125
  education, 6, 19
  income, 28
  in labor force, 6, 26
  poverty and, 28
  rights granted to, after Civil War, 12
  single mothers, 25
  voting behavior, 91
Blair, Diane D., 151
Blanco, Kathleen, 133
Blocker, T. Jean, 34
Boles, Janet, 152